Small- and Medium-Scale Industries in the ASEAN Countries

Westview Replica Editions

The concept of Westview Replica Editions is a response to the continuing crisis in academic and informational publishing. Library budgets for books have been severely curtailed. Ever larger portions of general library budgets are being diverted from the purchase of books and used for data banks, computers, micromedia, and other methods of information retrieval. Interlibrary loan structures further reduce the edition sizes required to satisfy the needs of the scholarly community. Economic pressures on the university presses and the few private scholarly publishing companies have severely limited the capacity of the industry to properly serve the academic and research communities. As a result, many manuscripts dealing with important subjects, often representing the highest level of scholarship, are no longer economically viable publishing projects--or, if accepted for publication, are typically subject to lead times ranging from one to three years.

Westview Replica Editions are our practical solution to the problem. We accept a manuscript in camera-ready form, typed according to our specifications, and move it immediately into the production process. As always, the selection criteria include the importance of the subject, the work's contribution to scholarship, and its insight, originality of thought, and excellence of exposition. The responsibility for editing and proofreading lies with the author or sponsoring institution. We prepare chapter headings and display pages, file for copyright, and obtain Library of Congress Cataloging in Publication Data. A detailed manual contains simple instructions for preparing the final typescript, and our editorial staff is always available to answer questions.

The end result is a book printed on acid-free paper and bound in sturdy library-quality soft covers. We manufacture these books ourselves using equipment that does not require a lengthy make-ready process and that allows us to publish first editions of 300 to 600 copies and to reprint even smaller quantities as needed. Thus, we can produce Replica Editions quickly and can keep even very specialized books in print as long as there is a demand for them.

About the Book and Authors

Small- and Medium-Scale Industries in the ASEAN Countries: Agents or Victims of Economic Development?

Mathias Bruch and Ulrich Hiemenz

Even though small- and medium-scale industries (SMIs) in developing countries are assumed to have great potential for generating income and employment, little is known about their actual performance. In this comparative study of SMIs in the five member countries of the Association of Southeast Asian Nations (ASEAN), Drs. Bruch and Hiemenz use data on performance of SMIs in the 1970s to show that they can significantly contribute to industrial growth and employment creation--but success is dependent on upgrading technology and adjusting product mix. They argue that traditional SMIs, which use simple technologies and produce simple consumer goods, must be replaced by enterprises that supply products for industrial use and manufacture export goods. Modernization, however, has been impeded by industrialization, trade, and credit policies that have favored the development of large-scale industries. The authors conclude that the viability of the SMI sector is critically dependent on changes in these restrictive policies and on programs to promote SMIs. They discuss the design of development policies that will create a macroeconomic environment in which SMIs can not only offer employment and income, particularly to less privileged sectors of the work force, but can also act as vital links in the chain of intra-industrial cooperation.

Mathias Bruch was a research fellow at the Kiel Institute of World Economics for eight years and is currently an officer for the Federal Ministry of Economics. He has written widely on the subject of small-scale establishments. Ulrich Hiemenz was formerly senior economist for the Asian Development Bank and is now head of development for the economics department of the Kiel Institute. He has written many publications on economic development and trade.

Small- and Medium-Scale Industries in the ASEAN Countries

Agents or Victims of Economic Development?

Mathias Bruch and Ulrich Hiemenz

Westview Press / Boulder and London

A Westview Replica Edition

Copyright © 1984 by Westview Press, Inc.

Published in 1984 in the United States of America by
   Westview Press, Inc.
   5500 Central Avenue
   Boulder, Colorado 80301
   Frederick A. Praeger, Publisher

Library of Congress Catalog Card Number: 84-50860
ISBN: 0-86531-848-4

Printed and bound in the United States of America
10 9 8 7 6 5 4 3 2

Contents

Tables

Preface

The role of small- and medium-scale industries (SMIs) in economic development has been given increased attention by both economists and policy makers in recent years. Unsatisfactory employment records of conventional industrialization strategies revived economic research on the smaller, labor-intensive units of production and induced many governments of developing countries to embark on special promotion programs. All these efforts have been hampered by a lack of detailed information on the characteristics of small-scale enterprises and an insufficient understanding of the interdependence between macroeconomic development strategies and sector-specific government intervention. The purpose of this study is to provide new insights into these important aspects of SMI development based on a comparative empirical analysis of the member countries of the Association of South East Asian Nations (ASEAN). The policy conclusions drawn in the study are addressed to economists and policy makers alike.

Work on the study was carried out in 1980-1982 at the Kiel Institute of World Economics (Kiel, West Germany) with financial support by the Stiftung Volkswagenwerk (VW Foundation). The completion of the study would have been impossible without the assistance provided by the government statistical offices of Malaysia, the Philippines and Singapore. We have also benefitted considerably from the advice of many government officials and economists from ASEAN countries to whom we owe our deep gratitude. The Asian Development Bank in Manila provided the opportunity to rewrite and supplement a first report on the project drafted in German. The final manuscript was completed in November 1983.

Finally, we should like to acknowledge the constant encouragement and constructive criticism of Herbert Giersch and Juergen B. Donges, Kiel Institute of World Economics, and of Seiji Naya and Madhab Godbole, Asian Development Bank. Barbara Buß had to bear with our many revisions in order to prepare the final manuscript.

Kiel, November 1983   *Mathias Bruch*
                                       Ulrich Hiemenz

1
Introduction

Part 1: Background and Focus of the Study

In the literature small- and medium-scale industries (SMIs) are generally considered to play an important role in economic development, both with respect to
employment creation and growth of income. SMIs are sup-
posed to have advantages over large-scale industries
(LIs) because:

- SMIs are labor-intensive and use relatively simple
  techniques of production that correspond to the abun-
  dance of labor and the scarcity of physical and human
  capital that prevail in most developing countries;
- SMIs demonstrate a higher degree of efficiency in
  using capital and in mobilizing savings, entrepreneurial talent and other resources that otherwise
  would remain idle.

It is further argued that SMIs can be efficient
suppliers to large establishments, and can satisfy
areas of demand neglected by large enterprises, thus
contributing to making manufacturing industries more
efficient, more flexible, and less prone to external
shocks.

Despite the development potential attributed to
SMIs, remarkably little is known about their performance compared with LIs, the macroeconomic consequences
of such performance differences, or the common determinants. Also, little research has been done regarding
policy formulation in the context of a global strategy
of industrialization. Main deficiencies in the literature on SMIs are lack of comparative analysis and con-
centration on SMI promotion policies with insufficient
regard being given to interdependencies on the sectoral
and macroeconomic levels.

The focus of this study is the interaction of
microlevel and macrolevel considerations and the pre-
sentation of a policy framework for the promotion of
SMIs consistent with a rational, comprehensive strategy
of industrialization. For the analysis, the experiences
of the member-countries of the Association of South

1

East Asian Nations (ASEAN) [1] were selected as empirical basis.

In the past two decades, industrialization has been emphasized in all ASEAN countries. Industrialization was originally perceived as an engine of productivity growth and income generation that would have favorable effects on the balance of payments through either import substitution or export diversification. This perception has gradually changed since the 1970s when it became evident that manufacturing was the most dynamic sector with respect to output growth, but the sector's performance in terms of generating employment and income has been quite uneven. Rising levels of unemployment and unsatisfactory rates of industrial employment creation drew the attention of most ASEAN governments to a better utilization of labor for industrial development. The new emphasis on growth-cum-employment strategies led to an increasing awareness of the development potential of SMIs, as is evident in the adoption of a number of SMI promotion programs in the 1970s.

To improve knowledge of the economic and policy environment in which SMIs can be induced to contribute to employment creation without sacrificing output growth, the objectives of the analysis are:

- to evaluate and compare the experiences of the five ASEAN countries with respect to the development of SMIs;
- to analyze the underlying economic forces that account for the inter-country differences in the relevant characteristics of SMIs as well as in their role in the process of industrialization;
- to provide criteria for the appropriate design of economic policies that are conducive to mobilizing the development potential of SMIs.

With these objectives, the focus of this study is distinguished from other studies on SMIs in two major respects: it is narrower than World Bank studies [2] insofar as analysis is limited to the ASEAN experience during the 1970s; within this scope, however, the approach is more comprehensive than those of the World Bank papers, an Asian Development Bank Occasional Paper [3], and a number of papers prepared by individual researchers [4]. While the previous studies focus mainly on the performance of SMIs in a static context and on the design of SMI promotion policies, this study bases policy conclusions on comparative evaluation of the overall economic environment of SMIs, macroeconomic as well as SMI-specific.

ASEAN countries are well suited for a study on the role of SMIs in economic development since the individual countries differ widely in their levels of economic development, their employment problems, and their economic policies, and in their geographical, social, and cultural situations. Examination of these differences is instrumental in assessing the impact of various factors on the economic and policy environments of SMIs in ASEAN countries. The results of such a comparative analysis will be relevant not only to ASEAN countries, but also to other countries with similar problems.

Part 2: Data Base and Conceptual Issues

Establishments of different sizes differ widely in areas such as technology, employment patterns, financing, market orientation, product characteristics, type of organization, and locational requirements. Despite its intuitively obvious meaning, the concept of plant size is inherently ambiguous as there are numerous criteria for measurement. In this study, the criterion of the number of persons engaged is used for two reasons: first, this is a comparative study and the number of persons engaged is the only dimension by which available data for different countries are disaggregated in a consistent way; and secondly, this variable normally correlates highly with other parameters such as value of output, capitalization, installed capacity, and energy consumption [5]. It is acknowledged that there may be capital-intensive establishments for which classification according to persons engaged obscures establishment size in terms of value added or capital investment, but as this study focuses on the analysis of industrial subsectors at the three-digit level of the International Standard Industrial Classification (ISIC), such exceptions are not likely to distort average, subsector-wide performance.

Although the characteristics of establishments will not change abruptly with changes in size, for analytical purposes it is necessary to define size classifications. The following disaggregation is widely accepted and has proved to be useful in a number of studies on developing countries:

1- 9	persons engaged:	Cottage and household industries (CIs)
10-49	persons engaged:	Small-scale industries (SIs)
50-99	persons engaged:	Medium-scale industries (MIs)
100+	persons engaged:	Large-Scale industries (LIs) [6].

This definition is based on the experience that in CIs, the owner normally is engaged in production, with management activities demanding only small amounts of time, that a considerable proportion of CI workers is family members, and that contacts with the outside world are mostly informal. SIs are characterized by

some division of labor, with the manager or entrepreneur not usually participating directly in the production process. In MIs, there is some formal organization
of activities and some specialization in management; in
LIs, this pattern is the norm [7].

The above definition of size groups is maintained
throughout the study as far as available data permit
[8]. It should be noted that this study will concen-
trate on establishments, not firms. Making such a distinction is not irrelevant as problems of access to
certain markets (e.g. institutional credit) and some
determinants of economies of scale are more a function
of firm size than establishment size. However, there is
evidence showing that independent establishments prevail at the lower end of the size spectrum.

The main source of data for an analysis of the
economic performance of SMIs is an industrial census.
In ASEAN countries, however, there are nearly no published sources of industrial census data simultaneously
disaggregated by plant size and by industry. The
national statistical offices of Indonesia, Malaysia,
the Philippines and Singapore agreed to undertake
special computer runs or to release unpublished ver-
sions of the required data; for Thailand, however, no
recent industrial census data are available and the
results of a sample survey [9] (1049 observations) are
used. These data are disaggregated only by plant size
or by industries, not by both criteria simultaneously.

Available data relate to those years in which
industrial censuses were conducted; the most recent
data refer to 1974/75 in Indonesia, 1973 in Malaysia,
1975 in the Philippines, and 1978 in Singapore. Comparisons over time are limited to census years, but coverage and industry classifications tend to differ substantially in industrial censuses from different years.
This deficiency precludes analysis of SMI development
in individual industrial subsectors for most ASEAN
countries, with the exception of Singapore. Growth and
employment in various size groups of establishments
can, however, be compared at the level of total manufacturing for Malaysia, 1963-73; the Philippines,
1961-75; and Singapore, 1963-78.

Part 3: Organization of the Study

The economic performance and the characteristics
of SMIs compared to CIs and LIs, in particular, are the
focal points of the first part of the study. In Chapter
2 the industrial plant size structures are compared
among ASEAN countries and changes of these structures
are traced over time. Aspects of employment generation
by industrial size groups and the relative efficiency
of factor use in SMIs and other plant size categories

are discussed in Chapter 3. Leading over to the second part of the study, the growth potential of the SMI sector is discussed in Chapter 4. The second part deals with the broader issue of how the characteristics, the competitive position, and the role of SMIs in economic development are influenced by the economic environment. How SMIs are affected by various policy measures is the subject of Chapters 5 and 6. In Chapter 5, macroeconomic industrialization policies of ASEAN countries are reviewed with respect to their impact on the development of the SMI sector. This impact of industrialization strategies pursued by individual countries is then contrasted with existing financial and nonfinancial programs promoting SMIs which are surveyed in Chapter 6. In its final part the study summarizes policy-induced and other bottlenecks to SMI development (Chapter 7) and discusses policy options for removing such bottlenecks (Chapter 8). A summary of main findings is presented in Chapter 9.

NOTES

1. These are Indonesia, Malaysia, the Philippines, Singapore and Thailand. Unless otherwise noted the term Malaysia used in this study refers to West Malaysia only.
2. World Bank (1978a); Marsden (1981); Anderson (1982).
3. van der Veen (1977).
4. See e.g. the various country studies prepared by staff members of the International Development Center of Japan.
5. See Shalit, Sankar (1977).
6. In some parts of this study the following subcategories are used: 100-199 persons engaged (LI1), and 200+ persons engaged (LI2).
7. See Staley (1958); Staley, Morse (1965, Chapter 1) for a discussion of a functional definition of SMIs.
8. Particularly with respect to cottage and household industries, different definitions are used occasionally since in some ASEAN countries the industrial census does not provide the required break down. The coverage of this size group is also incomplete as in the case of Singapore, where the industrial census provides data only for establishments engaging five or more persons.
9. See Tambunlertchai, Loohawenchit (1980).

2
Plant Size Structure:
Static and Dynamic Issues

Part 1: An International Comparison

In any country, a significant part of manufacturing takes place in small- and medium-scale enterprises; this is clearly demonstrated in Tables 2-1 and 2-2. In the United States, about 70 per cent of all establishments engaging five or more persons employed a total of fewer than 50 persons (1972); the respective figures are even more striking for other industrialized countries. In most developing countries, establishments engaging 5-49 persons account for about 90 per cent of all manufacturing establishments with five or more persons engaged. The quantitative importance of establishments engaging fewer than five persons can be seen from Table 2-2 [1]. Even in highly industrialized countries, at least one-half of all manufacturing establishments employ fewer than five persons; in developing countries this share can be well over 80 per cent.

With regard to long-term changes in the industrial plant size structure, the prevailing notion is that SMIs will decline relative to rising levels of economic development. The data presented in Table 2-1 indicate such a trend in the SMI share of manufacturing employment, but hardly in manufacturing value added; the SMI share in total manufacturing value added does not differ substantially between industrialized and developing countries. This implies that differences in labor productivity between establishments of different size are much more pronounced in developing countries than in industrialized countries.

Looking at the ASEAN countries more specifically, several general observations can be made (Table 2-3). In Indonesia and the Philippines, cottage and household industries appear to be extremely important in terms of their employment shares [2], but much less important in Malaysia and Singapore [3]. In Malaysia, the CI share in employment, value added, and the value of production is even smaller than in Japan, but still larger than in the United States. Once CIs are excluded from the anal-

Table 2-1: Relative Importance of SMIs in the Manufacturing Sector[a] of Selected Countries

Country[b] (Year)	GNP per capita 1976 (US $)	Persons engaged per establishment	Shares of establishments with 5-19, 5-49, and 5-99 persons engaged (per cent)								
			No. of establishments			Persons engaged			Value added		
			5-19	5-49	5-99	5-19	5-49	5-99	5-19	5-49	5-99
Low and Middle Income Countries											
Indonesia (1974/75)	240	20.1	85.5	94.8	97.4	32.3	45.4	54.1	9.6	17.6	25.7
Uganda (1971)	240	83.1	25.7	55.7	68.2	3.8	15.4	25.5	4.0c	13.8c	23.4c
Thailand (1964)	380	16.5	86.0	95.6	98.2	38.8	55.7	66.3	-	-	-
Philippines (1975)	410	33.1	-	91.1	94.5	-	28.0	35.4	-	8.6	14.4
Guatemala (1974)	630	35.3	71.6	87.5	-	18.9	54.1	-	7.0	39.8	-
Korea, South (1973)	670	49.7	72.3	85.9	91.8	12.1	20.4	28.8	5.6	10.2	16.9
Peru (1973)	800	43.9	63.4	82.9	91.2	13.3	26.7	39.9	5.0	14.9	26.2
Malaysia (1973)	860	58.8	52.4	77.2	88.1	10.9	25.4	38.4	6.1	16.7	31.1
Turkey (1970)	990	43.7	76.9	88.8	93.5	13.3	21.6	29.1	5.3	11.0	16.4
Taiwan (1971)d	1070	42.6	71.9	87.1	92.9	13.5	24.4	33.9	8.2	14.4	20.2
Mexico (1975)e	1090	65.7	61.6	76.2	87.0	10.5	18.3	29.7	5.7	11.1	20.2
Brazil (1970)	1140	38.8	68.5	86.0	93.0	15.9	29.6	41.9	9.1	19.4	30.3
Panama (1973)	1310	41.3	48.2	77.2	90.4	12.4	34.7	56.8	7.9	27.9	46.5
Venezuela (1974)	2570	40.6	65.2	85.2	92.4	16.5	32.1	44.6	7.1	15.8	26.7
Greece (1973)	2590	23.0	80.6	93.4	96.8	25.1	42.5	53.6	-	-	-
Singapore (1973)	2700	62.4	61.3	81.1	90.0	9.4	19.1	29.0	6.6	13.7	22.9
Israel (1972/73)	3920	36.5	71.5	87.8	93.9	17.8	31.6	43.3	12.5	25.3	37.1

Industrialized
Countries

Italy (1971)[f]	3050	40.4	65.7	86.1	93.5	16.2	31.4	44.0	–	–	–
New Zealand (1974)	4250	40.7	61.6	83.7	92.2	16.3	33.9	48.4	–	–	–
Japan (1973)	4910	30.5	76.0	90.6	95.6	23.0	38.0	49.5	14.4	26.0	35.4
Finland (1973)	5620	86.4	40.6	67.0	81.1	5.1	14.8	26.3	4.0	12.5	23.7
Belgium (1970)	6780	57.8	59.9	80.8	89.8	9.7	21.0	32.0	–	–	–
Germany (Federal Republic) (1970)	7380	58.6	66.5	83.1	90.5	9.9	18.7	27.6	–	–	–
Norway (1973)	7420	43.9	61.1	82.5	91.4	13.8	29.3	43.6	9.6	22.6	35.9
Denmark (1973)[f]	7450	63.9	43.9	74.2	86.9	7.8	22.3	36.1	–	–	–
Canada (1973)	7510	79.3	46.0	70.4	83.2	5.9	15.6	26.9	4.4	12.6	22.7
United States of America (1972)	7890	90.5	44.4	69.5	82.5	5.0	13.7	23.7	4.3	11.6	19.9

[a]Excluding CIs with 1-4 persons engaged. – [b]Grouping according to World Bank (1978b). – [c]Gross production at factor cost. – [d]4-19, 4-49, and 4-99 persons engaged. – [e]6-25, 6-50, 6-100 persons engaged. – [f]6-19, 6-49, and 6-99 persons engaged.

Source: World Bank, World Development Report 1978. Washington, D.C.; United Nations (UN) (1979), The 1973 World Programme of Industrial Statistics, Summary of Data from Selected Countries. New York; Secretaria de Planejamento da Presidência da República (SPPR) (1974), Censo Industrial Brasil, VIII Recenseamento Geral 1970, Série Nacional, Vol. IV, Rio de Janeiro; Secretaria de Programación y Presupuesto (SPP) (1979), X Censo Industrial 1976. Datos de 1975, Resumen General, Vol. I, Mexico, D.V.; Department of Statistics (Malaysia) (1973); Department of Statistics (Singapore) (1975); Committee on Industrial and Commercial Census of Taiwan and Fukien Area Executive Yuan (CICCT) (1973), The 1971 Industrial and Commercial Censuses of Taiwan and Fukien Area. Republic of China, Vol. III, Taipei; Biro Pusat Statistik (BPS) (Indonesia), 1974/75 Industrial Census. Jakarta, 1976-1978; National Statistical Office (NSO) (1968), Report on the 1964 Industrial Census. Bangkok; National Census and Statistics Office (NCSO) (1975), Summary Statistics of Manufacturing Establishments, Manila, unpublished.

Table 2-2: Relative Importance of CIs in the Manufacturing Sector
of Selected Countries

Country[a] (Year)	GNP p.cap. 1976 (US$)	Shares of establishments with 1-4 persons engaged (per cent)		
		establish- ments	No. of persons engaged	value added
Low and Middle Income Countries				
Indonesia (1974/75)	240	95.7	79.5	13.5
Thailand (1964)	380	91.9	55.5	–
Philippines (1975)	410	76.7	17.0	2.0
Korea, South (1973)	670	73.4	11.9	3.2
Peru (1973)	800	80.4	14.8	2.2
Malaysia (1973)	860	58.0	8.3	2.4
Turkey (1970)[b]	990	92.7	33.3	9.3
Mexico (1975)[b]	1090	80.6	11.2	2.9
Greece (1973)	2590	82.7	11.2	–
Industrialized Countries				
Italy (1971)[b]	3050	77.1	13.5	–
Japan (1973)	4910	48.6	7.1	2.7
Belgium (1970)	6780	66.6	5.9	–
Germany (Federal Republic) (1970)	7380	58.9	4.9	–

[a]Grouping according to World Bank (1978b). – [b]1-4 persons engaged.

Source: World Bank, World Development Report 1978. Washington, D.C.; United Nations (UN) (1979), The 1973 World Programme of Industrial Statistics, Summary of Data from Selected Countries. New York; Secretaria de Planejamento da Presidência da República (SPPR) (1974), Censo Industrial Brasil, VIII Recenseamento Geral 1970, Série Nacional, Vol. IV, Rio de Janeiro; Secretaria de Programación y Presupuesto (SPP) (1979), X Censo Industrial 1976. Datos de 1975, Resumen General, Vol. I, Mexico, D.V.; Department of Statistics (Malaysia) (1973); Department of Statistics (Singapore) (1975); Committee on Industrial and Commercial Census of Taiwan and Fukien Area Executive Yuan (CICCT) (1973), The 1971 Industrial and Commercial Censuses of Taiwan and Fukien Area. Republic of China, Vol. III, Taipei; Biro Pusat Statistik (BPS) (Indonesia), 1974/75 Industrial Census. Jakarta, 1976-1978; National Statistical Office (NSO) (1968), Report on the 1964 Industrial Census. Bangkok; National Census and Statistics Office (NCSO) (1975), Summary Statistics of Manufacturing Establishments, Manila, unpublished.

Table 2-3: ASEAN Countries and Selected Industrialized Countries - Size Structure of Total Manufacturing, Shares in per cent[a]

Country[b]	All establishments CIs	Establishments with 10 and more persons engaged		
		SIs	MIs	LIs
		No. of establishments		
Indonesia	98.7	83.9	8.2	7.9
Malaysia	64.4	71.4	14.1	14.5
Philippines	92.0	74.0	10.1	15.9
Singapore	-	72.4	13.1	14.5
Thailand[c]	63.8	81.5	10.5	8.0
Japan	74.5	81.0	10.1	8.9
USA	49.3	60.6	16.8	22.6
		Persons engaged[d]		
Indonesia	83.5	31.3	10.9	57.8
Malaysia	9.2	22.8	14.2	63.0
Philippines	27.4	17.7	8.4	73.9
Singapore	-	18.2	11.1	70.7
Thailand	-	-	-	-
Japan	17.4	30.3	12.9	56.8
USA	2.7	12.3	10.2	77.5
		Value added		
Indonesia	18.2	12.9	8.5	78.6
Malaysia	3.7	15.2	14.4	70.4
Philippines	4.0	6.8	5.9	87.3
Singapore	-	13.1	8.9	78.0
Thailand	-	-	-	-
Japan	8.7	21.1	10.0	68.9
USA	2.5	10.3	8.5	81.2
		Value of Production		
Indonesia	16.8	14.5	10.5	75.0
Malaysia	4.1	18.2	14.7	67.1
Philippines	3.4	7.7	6.8	85.5
Singapore	-	11.4	6.8	81.8
Thailand	-	-	-	-
Japan	6.7	20.0	10.3	69.7
USA	2.3	10.2	8.9	80.9

[a]For definition of size groups see Ch. .2. Shares of SIs, MIs, and LIs add up to 100 per cent. See footnote 1, p. 11. - [b]Indonesia 1974/75, Malaysia 1973, Philippines 1975, Singapore 1978, Thailand 1976, Japan 1973, USA 1972. - [c]Based on sample survey (N = 1094). [d]Average of establishments with 10+ persons engaged: Indonesia: 49.5, Malaysia: 68.6, Philippines: 84.6, Singapore: 82.7, Japan: 30.5, USA: 115.1.

Source: United Nations (UN) (1979), The 1973 World Programme of Industrial Statistics, Summary of Data from Selected Countries. New York; Biro Pusat Statistik (BPS) (Indonesia), 1974/75 Industrial Census. Jakarta, 1976-1978; Department of Statistics (Malaysia) (1973); National Census and Statistics Office (NCSO) (1975), Summary Statistics of Manufacturing Establishments, Manila, unpublished; Department of Statistics (Singapore) (1979); Tambunlertchai, Loohawenchit (1980).

ysis, it is found that the SI share in employment and
in value added is far smaller in the ASEAN countries,
with the exception of Indonesia, than in Japan. This
situation is especially pronounced for the Philippines,
where the SI share in value added is even less than in
the United States. This is also the case for MIs in the
Philippines. Manufacturing in this country can be considered an example of a highly dualistic sector with a
large number of labor-intensive CIs on one side, and a
large LI subsector on the other. Quite differently, SIs
and MIs are well-represented in the Malaysian manufacturing sector. Because of her many labor-intensive LIs,
Singapore takes an intermediate position. In Indonesia,
the LI share in employment is relatively low, but in
value added it is relatively high. The differences in
the importance of the SMI sector among ASEAN countries
do not only reflect different levels of economic development but also different degrees of competitiveness of
small-scale versus large-scale enterprises in the
specific economic environments.

Part 2: Small and Large Establishments in
        ASEAN Countries

(a) Determinants of Plant Size Structure

Small- and medium-scale industries are far from
being a homogenous group; SMIs differ by criteria such
as the level of technology employed, location, use of
raw materials and other inputs, product characteristics
and output markets. All these factors have some significance in the coexistence of small and large establishments in the same industrial subsectors. Based on these
criteria, the following types of relationships between
small and large establishments can be distinguished:

(1) Production for local markets: A number of goods
    must be produced locally, either because they are
    perishable or because their transportation is
    rather costly (some food products, construction
    materials, custom tailoring). With respect to
    such goods, small local producers enjoy some
    degree of "natural" protection against LIs.
(2) Processing of spatially dispersed raw materials:
    Small producers have cost advantages over large
    producers if the processing of spatially dis-
    persed raw materials results in a reduction of
    bulkiness or risk of spoilage and, thus, of
    transport costs.
(3) Traditional craft products: The special character
    of these products is a result of (simple) tradi-
    tional production techniques. Economies of scale
    in such activities are decreasing or constant;

they do not provide cost advantages to large-scale production.

(4) Technological heterogeneity: A number of manufactured goods can be produced using either simple or relatively sophisticated techniques. As has been shown elsewhere, SMIs can successfully compete with LIs in a number of industries if intermediate, labor-intensive techniques are used μ 4#; SMIs can thus at least partially offset some of the disadvantages inherent in their small size such as market instability, problems of access to financial sources, and lack of appropriate infrastructure. Furthermore, simple techniques can be operated with cheaper, low-skilled labor.

(5) Size-specific product differentiation: Many SMIs owe their existence not only to technological heterogeneity, but also to the fact that they do not compete directly with LIs in producing the same goods. Examples of such differentiation are production of inferior substitutes for consumer goods for lower income groups, or production of luxury items. Another factor that may help SMIs compete with LIs is their greater flexibility in serving the special needs of individual customers.

(6) Size-specific vertical specialization: SMIs may have cost advantages in the production of simple components, in the provision of industrial services, or in the assembly of highly diversified but standardized components. The supply of these inputs to LIs can be crucial for the international competitiveness of LIs and, hence, for successful industrial development.

Some of the reasons for the coexistence of SMIs and LIs are more significant in some subsectors than in others, but the relative importance of these factors as determinants of the plant size structure is also influenced by development policies, the situation in the labor market, infrastructural conditions, etc. Therefore, the size structure of manufacturing establishments does not only differ between individual industries, but also in the same industry operating in different countries.

(b)   Inter-Industry Differences

Detailed information on the size structure of industrial establishments in ASEAN countries is contained in Table 2-4. Comparing the average number of persons engaged per establishment in individual industries and in the total manufacturing sectors (excluding CIs) of ASEAN countries, it is revealed that average

Table 2-4: ASEAN Countries[a] - Size Structure of Manufacturing Industries, Shares in per cent[b,c]

Industry (ISIC)[d] Country	Persons engaged					Value of production			
	All establishments	Establishments with 10+ persons engaged				All establishments	Establishments with 10+ persons engaged		
	CIs	SIs	MIs	LIs	Average[e]	CIs	SIs	MIs	LIs
Food processing (311 + 312)									
IND	89.4	37.4	9.0	53.6	41.7	32.7	22.5	13.1	64.4
MAl	20.5	32.3	12.8	54.9	50.3	6.6	27.1	13.3	59.6
PHI	40.3	20.0	5.9	74.1	73.2	5.7	7.9	5.6	86.5
SIN	-	40.7	18.7	40.6	37.9	-	38.1	16.2	45.7
Beverages (313)									
IND	52.0	44.8	9.6	45.6	33.9	4.5	7.2	5.0	87.8
MAL	3.5	20.5	24.1	55.4	41.9	0.7	5.0	13.5	81.5
PHI	4.7	3.9	2.6	93.5	306.2	0.3	2.9	2.8	94.2
SIN	-	-	-	-	185.4	-	-	-	-
Tobacco (314)									
IND	10.3	8.9	7.3	83.8	154.1	1.3	2.0	2.0	96.0
MAL	2.0	25.8	25.0	49.2	70.4	0.3	2.8	3.0	94.2
PHI	0.0	0.7	3.7	95.6	522.1	0.0	0.3	0.6	99.1
SIN	-	-	-	-	157.9	-	-	-	-
Textiles (321)									
IND	67.9	33.6	12.6	53.8	48.6	6.7	19.2	13.8	67.0
MAL	2.1	5.0	4.9	90.1	212.1	1.4	4.7	2.9	92.4
PHI	10.6	7.1	6.3	86.6	171.6	1.8	5.8	9.6	84.6
SIN	-	8.4	10.0	81.6	122.6	-	10.6	9.9	79.5
Clothing (322)									
IND[f]	86.4	72.1	12.3	15.6	23.0	67.4	78.4	11.4	10.2
MAL[f]	3.0	20.1	9.1	68.8	81.9	3.0	23.0	13.1	63.9
PHI	67.0	18.0	6.8	75.2	72.0	37.8	16.0	12.3	71.7
SIN	-	17.1	11.0	71.9	84.0	-	17.5	9.3	73.2
Leather and l. products (323)									
IND	73.0	46.6	22.3	31.1	33.5	23.7	41.9	14.6	43.5
MAL	16.7	45.0	40.4	14.6	38.2	8.5	50.5	45.3	4.2
PHI	25.7	32.4	20.7	46.9	47.3	6.3	23.3	19.3	57.4
SIN	-	53.1	46.9	-	30.7	-	64.2	35.8	-
Footwear (324)									
IND	56.9	35.2	4.9	59.9	69.0	20.9	18.1	3.5	78.4
MAL	22.3	39.2	20.6	40.2	37.5	19.1	33.4	16.6	50.0
PHI	57.0	64.6	7.7	27.7	26.0	40.2	51.5	7.6	40.9
SIN	-	55.9		44.1	32.4	-	70.2		29.8
Wood and cork products (331)									
IND	98.1	55.2	11.6	32.2	.28.2	52.7	31.5	11.3	57.2
MAL	3.7	23.5	20.9	55.6	69.9	2.0	24.5	25.4	50.1
PHI	13.3	14.1	8.3	77.6	102.5	5.0	18.2	13.3	68.5
SIN	-	23.2	11.6	65.2	75.8	-	22.6	12.9	64.5
Furniture (332)									
IND	93.3	80.7	7.7	11.6	18.1	72.5	66.2	10.7	23.1
MAL	43.2	59.1	22.3	18.6	26.5	29.5	50.6	22.3	27.1
PHI	40.3	46.9	21.3	31.8	33.4	27.8	50.1	24.8	25.1
SIN	-	26.4	22.0	51.6	50.0	-	36.6	21.8	41.6
Paper and p. products (341)									
IND	40.3	19.6	6.7	73.7	87.8	2.5	4.8	2.5	92.7
MAL	8.9	28.3	14.8	56.9	52.1	5.7	23.5	11.8	64.7
PHI	3.5	13.8	8.9	77.3	103.7	1.2	10.1	6.7	83.2
SIN	-	34.5	33.8	31.7	44.2	-	30.2	31.7	28.0
Printing and publishing (342)									
IND	28.5	44.9	16.2	38.9	35.6	10.1	36.3	21.6	42.1
MAL	6.3	38.1	15.4	46.5	46.8	4.4	28.3	16.5	55.2
PHI	21.3	47.8	17.2	35.0	35.7	6.9	29.1	14.9	56.0
SIN	-	39.1	11.2	49.7	42.5	-	33.4	11.7	54.9
Industrial chemicals (351)									
IND	-	19.8	16.5	63.7	70.4	-	7.8	12.8	79.4
MAL	1.5	25.2	14.9	59.9	69.2	4.3	34.2	15.5	50.2
PHI	0.8	21.1	13.6	65.3	86.5	0.4	16.8	15.4	67.8
SIN	-	-	-	-	60.1	-	-	-	-
Other chemicals (352)									
IND	27.0	21.8	14.1	64.0	67.0	4.2	13.5	13.4	73.0
MAL	9.5	25.2	14.9	59.9	58.7	3.8	19.5	18.2	62.3
PHI	1.7	10.8	15.3	73.9	113.6	0.2	8.4	13.5	78.1
SIN	-	38.2	23.6	38.2	42.8	-	24.4	13.4	62.2

continued

Table 2-4

Industry (ISIC) Country[d]	Persons engaged					Value of production			
	All establishments	Establishments with 10+ persons engaged				All establishments	Establishments with 10+ persons engaged		
	CIs	SIs	MIs	LIs	Average[e]	CIs	SIs	MIs	MIs
Rubber products (355)									
IND	14.1	18.4	16.9	64.7	77.4	1.2	8.8	13.7	77.6
MAL	5.7	9.8	12.3	77.9	118.3	2.0	8.0	20.6	71.4
PHI	7.4	11.4	9.9	78.7	113.0	1.7	4.4	3.1	92.5
SIN	-	-	-	-	65.1	-	-	-	-
Plastic products (356)									
IND	40.8	37.4	19.5	43.1	41.3	11.1	36.1	21.9	42.0
MAL	7.7	29.3	14.9	55.8	54.3	5.7	34.7	20.6	44.7
PHI	3.7	16.7	13.5	69.8	90.7	1.8	20.2	14.8	65.0
SIN	-	37.7	28.6	33.7	44.9	-	39.0	28.1	32.9
Pottery, china, earthenware (361)									
IND	97.7	57.2	13.4	29.4	28.9	66.8	82.8	4.8	12.4
MAL	10.1	36.5	0.0	63.5	39.5	3.1	14.3	0.0	85.7
PHI	28.4	10.9	0.0	89.1	103.2	1.6	4.6	0.0	95.4
SIN	-	-	-	-	-	-	-	-	-
Glass and glass products (362)									
IND	-	12.5	10.7	76.8	104.8	-	5.9	2.3	91.8
MAL	5.7	2.7	3.6	93.7	181.4	5.4	10.5	0.1	89.4
PHI	2.2	5.3	0.0	92.6	236.6	1.7	9.5	0.0	90.5
SIN	-	-	-	-	-	-	-	-	-
Other non-metallic mineral products (369)									
IND	86.8	71.8	9.3	18.9	21.3	37.8	28.9	7.5	63.6
MAL	5.1	31.6	23.4	45.0	56.1	2.0	13.3	11.3	75.4
PHI	24.8	21.5	7.1	71.4	79.2	3.4	5.5	5.2	89.3
SIN	-	30.9		69.1	60.6	-	32.1		67.9
Basic metals (371 + 372)									
IND	-	-	-	-	-	-	-	-	-
MAL	8.6	18.9	6.9	74.2	83.7	3.7	13.6	11.6	74.8
PHI	-	12.5	16.9	70.6	102.9	-	3.6	16.8	79.6
SIN	-	-	-	-	93.3	-	-	-	-
Metal products (381)									
IND	69.5	33.8	12.6	53.6	43.0	16.7	14.4	16.5	69.0
MAL	18.8	29.5	18.9	51.6	50.8	8.5	22.9	19.2	57.9
PHI	26.4	28.9	6.7	64.4	61.8	5.0	20.3	8.5	71.2
SIN	-	32.1	21.2	46.7	48.1	-	31.8	20.1	48.1
Non-electrical machinery (382)									
IND	-	23.2	10.1	66.7	67.2	-	9.1	15.9	75.0
MAL	16.2	45.4	22.2	32.4	36.5	10.3	34.2	24.6	41.2
PHI	12.5	36.4	18.1	45.5	48.1	5.8	19.8	20.8	59.4
SIN	-	20.9	11.1	68.0	69.4	-	18.0	10.9	71.1
Electrical machinery (383)									
IND	-	7.8	10.4	81.8	141.7	-	4.5	5.0	90.5
MAL	0.3	3.3	3.2	93.5	275.1	0.5	3.2	5.9	90.9
PHI	1.3	9.1	5.2	85.7	147.9	0.6	6.0	4.3	89.7
SIN	-	3.9	4.7	91.4	275.3	-	2.7	3.6	93.7
Transport equipment (384)									
IND	31.1	20.4	9.8	69.8	71.8	1.7	4.1	5.0	90.9
MAL	4.5	15.6	7.4	77.0	99.0	1.7	7.3	7.1	85.6
PHI	8.4	22.9	13.5	63.6	71.2	1.5	6.5	7.8	85.7
SIN	-	11.7	4.1	84.2	129.6	-	8.0	3.5	88.5
Professional goods, etc. (385)									
IND	-	71.6	15.3	13.1	24.6	-	79.7	16.9	3.6
MAL	3.1	5.5	12.0	82.5	151.0	1.1	4.1	14.8	81.1
PHI	9.0	14.0	12.2	73.8	89.4	15.2	9.2	11.7	79.1
SIN	-	11.3		88.7	214.0	-	14.1		85.9
Other manufacturing (390)									
IND	90.5	47.5	8.7	43.8	31.9	50.0	34.7	11.1	54.2
MAL	17.2	35.0	15.8	49.2	46.6	10.0	40.8	8.7	50.5
PHI	26.6	67.2	12.9	19.9	26.1	10.5	63.1	16.7	20.2
SIN	-	40.4	14.1	45.6	47.9	-	52.1	18.0	29.9

[a]Without Thailand. - [b]For definition of size groups see Chapter 1.2. Shares of SIs, MIs, and LIs add up to 100. See footnote 2 in Chapter 2. - [c]Above average values (relative to those in Table 2-3) are underlined. - [d]Indonesia 1974/75, Malaysia 1973, Philippines 1975, Singapore 1978. - [e]Average no. per establishment. - [f]Without small tailoring shops.

Source: United Nations (UN) (1979), The 1973 World Programme of Industrial Statistics, Summary of Data from Selected Countries. New York. - Biro Pusat Statistik (BPS) (Indonesia), 1974/75 Industrial Census. Jakarta, 1976-1978. - Department of Statistics (Malaysia) (1973). - National Census and Statistics Office (NCSO) (1975), Summary Statistics of Manufacturing Establishments, Manila, unpublished. - Department of Statistics (Singapore) (1979). - Tambunlertchai, Loohawenchit (1980).

plant size differs substantially between manufacturing industries in all countries. Judged from the average number of persons engaged smaller establishments play an important role in food, leather, and furniture industries, in printing and publishing, and in "other manufacturing" industries [5]. On the other hand, average size is relatively large in the tobacco, glass, basic metals and electrical machinery industries. In the quantitatively important textile and clothing industries, average plant size is relatively low in Indonesia and to some extent in the Philippines, but not in the other two countries.

The relative importance of individual size groups becomes apparent when the percentage shares in employment and in the value of production for establishments of different sizes are compared. Table 2-4 shows that CIs are concentrated in several industries where traditional techniques of production are available and competitive under present conditions. In the three countries for which data are available, CIs are concentrated mainly in the food, furniture and pottery industries, as measured by their employment shares. Other industries with a fairly high share of CI employment are clothing, footwear, leather, wood and metal products. CIs are virtually nonexistent in the production of tobacco products, industrial chemicals, basic metals, electrical machinery and professional goods.

Contrary to the general case of CIs, SIs are less concentrated in specific manufacturing industries. Nevertheless, a number of industries in which SIs have above-average employment shares can be identified in at least three of the four countries under observation. These are industries which produce goods using relatively simple, labor-intensive techniques (like leather, footwear, furniture, or metal products, or "other" manufactures) or process spatially dispersed raw materials (like food and wood products), or industries in which proximity to the markets is important (as in the food and printing industries). In the textiles industry, a large difference between countries can be observed; large-scale textile mills predominate in Malaysia, the Philippines and in Singapore, while in Indonesia simple weaving techniques in SIs are still important. Similar differences between countries can be observed in the clothing industry.

In all countries, LIs prevail in "modern" industries or industries characterized by significant economies of scale, such as the production of electrical machinery, transport equipment and rubber, glass, and tobacco products, but compared to other size groups, their sectoral production pattern is less specialized. Judged from sectoral employment shares, LIs play an important role in almost all manufacturing subsectors in each ASEAN country, while SMIs have substantial

employment shares in only a few industries. This pattern emerges from the coefficients of variation
presented in Table 2-5. In the four ASEAN countries
shown in Table 2-5, with few minor exceptions the
variation of employment shares declines with increasing
plant size.

Table 2-5 : ASEAN Countries - Coefficients of Variation for the
Employment Shares of Individual Size Groups among
Industries

Establishment size groups (persons engaged)	Indonesia	Malaysia	Philip- pines	Singapore
CIs: 1 - 9	0.76	0.96	1.04	–
SIs: 10 - 49	0.56	0.55	0.80	0.55
MIs: 50 - 99	0.35	0.58	0.59	0.66
LIs: 100+	0.44	0.35	0.32	0.44

Source: United Nations (UN) (1979), The 1973 World Programme of
Industrial Statistics, Summary of Data from Selected Countries.
New York; Biro Pusat Statistik (BPS) Indonesia, 1974/75 Industrial
Census. Jakarta, 1976-1978; Department of Statistics (Malaysia)
(1973); National Census and Statistics Office (NCSO) (1975),
Summary Statistics of Manufacturing Establishments, Manila,
unpublished; Department of Statistics (Singapore) (1979);
Tambunlertchai, Loohawenchit (1980).

(c)   Inter-Country Differences

Analysis has so far shown significant similarities
between ASEAN countries with respect to the shares of
SMIs in manufacturing industries. There are, however,
significant differences. It has been argued in Section
2.2. (a) that the basic determinants of plant size
structure will not be the same in all countries, nor
will they be independent of levels of economic development and applied industrialization strategies. Hence,
there are differences between individual countries in
the plant size structure as well as in the change of
this structure over time.

The displacement of traditional crafts by intermediate and modern technology is a common phenomenon in
economic development. As national, regional and local
markets are opened up by improved transportation infrastructure, many traditional industries are driven out
of their markets by imports or by more efficient domestic suppliers. The displacement of traditional suppliers is slow, however, in such countries as Indonesia

and the Philippines, which are archipelagos. In these countries, high transportation costs provide "natural" protection to producers in rural areas and outlying islands. It is not surprising that in the 1970s employment in CIs still constitutes the bulk of industrial employment in both countries. The Indonesian Industrial Census of 1974/75 shows that employment in CIs accounted for more than 80 per cent of total manufacturing employment, while the respective figure for the Philippines was about 53 per cent [6].

In Indonesia, as well as the Philippines, production for local markets is concentrated in traditional CIs to a much greater degree than in Malaysia and in Singapore; this is evident in relatively high CI employment shares in Indonesia and the Philippines in industries such as food, textiles, clothing, leather, pottery and earthenware, and "other" nonmetallic mineral products (Table 2-4). Similar considerations are also relevant for SI employment shares, especially in Indonesia, where CIs as well as SIs largely use traditional technology and are often located in rural areas. This can help to explain the high SI employment shares in industries such as beverages, textiles, and clothing.

Another common phenomenon in economic development is the unequal diffusion of technical progress among establishments of different sizes [7]. The application of modern and mostly capital-intensive techniques of production is the rule among LIs, while SIs and MIs tend to use intermediate technology; CIs are mostly traditional. The causes for an unequal diffusion of technical progress are related to economic environments of SMIs and relevant economic policies. Conditions in the labor market, in particular wide-spread un- and underemployment, will be clearly reflected in the size of the CI sector, where entry is easy, while economic policies favoring the use of physical capital or large-scale production impede development of SIs and MIs.

"Natural" protection through transport costs cannot be the only reason for the persistence of CIs, as they are also fairly well represented in urban areas of Indonesia and the Philippines. An important reason for the continued importance of CIs in these two countries appears to be the acute employment situation. A common experience in most developing countries is that after industrialization began, usually during colonial times, increasing efforts were made to substitute domestically manufactured goods for imported products. In this phase, policies tended to promote the application of modern imported technology in capital-intensive LIs, which are either vertically integrated to a high degree or highly dependent on imported intermediate inputs. High wages and low labor absorption in the modern industrial sectors are features of this type of industrialization which has been predominant in both Indonesia and the Philippines throughout the 1970s. When the agricultural sector could not provide sufficient employment opportunities, many of the unemployed or under-employed resorted to informal activities, such as CIs, where entry usually is easy but incomes are low.

The influence of the labor market situation can be traced by comparing the plant size structure in Indonesia and the Philippines to that in Malaysia and Singapore. In the case of Indonesia, regional income data suggest that the share of CIs in industrial employment has remained about constant in the 1970s, implying the same rates of labor absorption for CIs as for larger manufacturing industries [8]. This means that in the 1970s more than 80 per cent of the industrial labor force continued to be employed in CIs (Table 2-3). Estimates by Anderson and Khambata [9] for the Philippines show that household industries experienced a mild but steady decline in their employment shares since 1961, but that employment in very small establishments (fewer than ten persons engaged) grew even faster than total manufacturing employment (Table 2-6). Hence, both types of industries taken together still employed more than 65 per cent of the industrial labor force in 1975.

In Malaysia and Singapore, household industries and very small establishments accounted for about half of manufacturing (57 and 48 per cent respectively in 1963, see Table 2-7), when the employment problem was still pressing in these two countries. In the favorable international economic environment of the late 1960s and early 1970s, both governments embarked on more outward-looking industrial policies and attracted large volumes of export-oriented direct foreign investment. The employment problem was thereby reduced in Malaysia and practically resolved in Singapore. As a result, employment creation shifted substantially from low-income occupations, such as in CIs, to more remunerative jobs in larger establishments. As can be seen from Table 2-7, employment in household industries and very small establishments declined in both countries after 1963 even in absolute numbers while total manufacturing employment increased rapidly.

While the availability of cheap labor has sustained high employment shares in CIs and traditional SIs, other environmental factors were less favorable for SMIs using intermediate technology and producing more advanced products. The shares of these nontraditional SMIs declined both with respect to industrial employment and industrial value added in almost all ASEAN countries (Table 2-8). Given the rapid pace of industrialization, this finding contradicts general expectations. Standard theory suggests that small establishments compete with LIs in the production of consumer goods at an early stage of economic development. In the

Table 2-6: Philippines - Employment in Manufacturing by Establishment Size, 1961-1975

Establishment size (Persons en-gaged)	1961	1967	1972	1975	Average annual growth rates (per cent)	
					1967-75	1961-75
No. of persons engaged (in 1000)						
Household industries	665	871	839	882	0.2	2.0
Establishments						
1 - 9	96	125	204	207	6.5	5.6
10 - 19		23	27	37	6.1	)
20 - 99	267	65	69	95	4.9	) 5.5
100 - 199		38	43	56	5.0	)
200+		268	285	374	4.3	)
Total	1028	1390	1467	1651	2.2	3.4

	Relative shares (per cent)				Survival coefficients[a]	
					1975/1967	1975/1961
Household industries	64.7	62.7	57.2	53.4	0.85	0.83
Establishments						
1 - 9	9.3	9.0	13.9	12.5	1.39	1.34
10 - 19		1.7	1.8	2.2	1.29	)
20 - 99	26.0	4.7	4.7	5.8	1.23	) 1.31
100 - 199		2.7	2.9	3.4	1.26	)
200+		19.3	19.4	22.7	1.18	)
Total	100.0	100.0	100.0	100.0	1.00	1.00

[a] Share of 1975/share of 1967 (or 1961 resp.).

Source: Anderson, Khambata (1981, p. 80).

Table 2-7: Malaysia and Singapore - Employment in Household Industries and in Establishments with Less Than 5 Persons
Engaged (in 1000), 1959-1978[a]

	1959	1963	1968	1973	1978	GR[b] 1973/68
Malaysia						
Employment in manufacturing (1)	166.0	190.0	238.0	344.0	–	7.6
Employment in household industries (Share in (1), per cent)	99.4 (59.9)	88.6 (46.6)	91.9 (38.6)	46.1 (13.4)	– –	-12.9
Employment in household industries and in establish- ments with less than 5 paid full- time employees (Share in (1), per cent)	106.0 (63.9)	108.9 (57.3)	102.3 (43.0)	70.2 (20.4)	– –	-7.3
Singapore						
Employment in manufacturing (2)	–	79.0	105.0	226.5	270.6	16.6
Employment in household industries and in establish- ments with less than 5 persons engaged (Share in (2), per cent)	–	37.7 (47.7)	22.9 (21.8)	19.0 (8.4)	18.1 (6.7)	-3.7

[a] Employment in household industries has been estimated as the
difference between total employment in manufacturing and employment as recorded in the industrial censuses. Deficient coverage in
the Malaysian Census of Manufacturing Industries of 1959 has been
corrected by adding 5 per cent of the recorded figure. Figures for
total employment in manufacturing are a result of nonlinear inter-
polation based on Tan (1979, p. 103); Department of Statistics
(Singapore, 1980); Yin, Clark (1976, pp. 238 ff).

[b] Average annual growth rate (per cent).

Sources: Department of Statistics (Malaysia, 1959, 1963, 1968,
1973), Census of Manufacturing Industries, Peninsular Malaysia.
Kuala Lumpur. - Department of Statistics (Singapore, 1963, 1968,
1973, 1978, 1980), Report on the Census of Industrial Production.
Singapore. - Tan (1979, p. 103); Yin, Clark (1976, pp. 328 ff.).

Table 2-8: Value Added Growth and Employment Creation by Size of
            Establishment in Selected ASEAN Countries - Average
            Annual Growth Rates (per cent)

Country/ Year	Value added growth[a]				Employment creation[b]			
	Persons engaged per establishment				Persons engaged per establishment			
	10-49	50-99	100+	10+	10-49	50-99	100+	10+
Malaysia								
1968/63	7.2	-4.5	39.3	15.8	3.7	7.9	14.9	8.3
1973/68	16.1	22.3	24.1	21.6	9.2	13.1	23.7	16.9
1973/63	11.6	8.7	31.5	18.7	6.4	10.5	19.2	12.5
Philippines								
1975/67	3.7	9.5	19.0	16.8	5.5	4.3	3.7	4.6
Singapore								
1968/63	17.5	18.7	20.5	18.8	12.0	13.7	19.3	14.7
1973/68	16.8	10.4	43.7	32.5	3.1	7.9	33.8	20.4
1978/73	17.0	14.1	15.1	15.2	7.6	5.7	3.2	4.0
1978/63	17.1	14.3	25.9	21.9	7.5	9.1	18.1	12.8

[a] Current prices. - [b] Employment refers to paid employees only in
the case of Malaysia. In all other countries employment is measured by the total number of workers.

Sources: Department of Statistics (Malaysia, 1963, 1968, 1973);
University of the Philippines Institute for Small-Scale Industries
(UPISSI), A Study on Philippine Small- and Medium-Scale Industries, Phase I. Quezon City, November 1977 and unpublished material; Department of Statistics (Singapore, 1963, 1968, 1973,
1978).

course of successful industrialization, however, markets become more integrated and the demand for traditional consumer goods shows a relative decline, as demand in general becomes more diversified. These more developed markets create opportunities for product differentiation and division of labor between establishments of different sizes. SMIs can expand into the production of goods with high income elasticities and can qualify as suppliers to LIs. Such a shift of the industrial structure toward complementary relationships between small and large establishments did, however, hardly take place in ASEAN countries.

In both Indonesia and the Philippines, SIs have remained largely traditional in character. In Indonesia, the SI share in manufacturing employment is comparatively high, while it is rather low in manufacturing value added reflecting a very low labor productivity in the large SI sector. Low productivity of SIs and the small shares of the MI sector suggest that the economic climate in Indonesia was rather more conducive to the establishment and growth of LIs than of nontraditional SMIs. A similar picture emerges in the case of the Philippines. Employment in SMIs has expanded faster than total manufacturing employment in this country in 1967-1975 (Table 2-8), but value added growth badly lagged behind that of LIs; SMI shares in manufacturing employment and value added remained small (Table 2-3).

In Malaysia and Singapore, average labor productivity in SMIs is substantially higher than in the other two countries indicating the relative importance of nontraditional SMIs in these countries; however, their share in manufacturing employment and value added declined, too, both in 1963-1968 and in 1968-1973. It seems reasonable to assume that this relative decline was related to the promotion of capital-intensive LIs through import substitution policies in Malaysia, particularly in the 1963-1968 period, and to the inflow of foreign direct investment into large-scale, labor-intensive export industries in both Malaysia and Singapore.

The relationship of economic policies and SMI performance will be assessed later in this study. At this stage of the analysis it should be sufficient to stress that a declining SMI sector is not a natural phenomenon of economic growth. This was already demonstrated by international comparisons of plant size structures in developing and industrializing countries, but it can also be shown with respect to development over time in individual countries such as in Singapore. Table 2-8 shows for this country that since 1973 especially larger SIs were able to increase their shares in manufacturing employment and value added. As has been observed elsewhere [10], between 1973 and 1978 SMIs oriented toward providing industrial services such as electro-plating, heat-treatment and polishing showed the highest growth rates. This successful performance seems to indicate a shift of the industrial structure toward the complementary relationship between small and large establishments suggested by economic theory.

NOTES

1. For many countries, data relating to very small establishments are either not available or are unreliable. Table 2-1 has thus been confined to manufacturing establishments with five or more persons engaged.

2. It should be noted that in Table 2-3 as well as in all other similar tables, the shares of CIs refer to all establishments while the shares of larger establishments refer only to establishments with ten or more persons, engaged. Thus, only the shares of SIs, MIs, and LIs add up to 100 per cent; otherwise the size structure of establishments with ten or more persons engaged would have become unduly biased by the large variation among CI shares and by the differing coverage of CIs in the respective industrial censuses.

3. In the case of Singapore this is suggested by a comparison of data for establishments with more than four persons engaged but fewer than ten. The data for Thailand in Table 2-3 are based on establishments registered with the Factory Control Division. In this case coverage is especially deficient for very small establishments. For details see Tambunlertchai, Loohawenchit (1980).

4. See Bruch (1982c, Chapter 3). Technological heterogeneity refers to nonhomothetic production functions. In such functions several efficient factor combinations may exist for any given factor price ratio. This possibility is discussed further in Chapter 3.3.

5. The ISIC category "other manufacturing" includes, inter alia, the production of musical instruments, toys, and pens and pencils. SMIs are traditionally major producers of these goods.

6. While the data relating to CIs in Indonesia seem to reflect the correct order of magnitude, a large part of household industries has not been covered in the Industrial Census of the Philippines. For an independent estimate, see Anderson, Khambata (1981, p. 80).

7. See e.g. Nelson, Schultz, Slighton (1971).

8. See McCawley, Tait (1979, p. 136).

9. Anderson, Khambata (1981, p. 80).

10. See Bruch (1982c).

3
Contribution to Employment, Output, and Income Generation

Part 1: Basic Characteristics of
        Establishments of Different Size

The unsatisfactory growth performance of SMIs in most ASEAN countries calls for a more rigorous analysis of the contributions which establishments of different size can make to various objectives of economic development such as employment, output, and income generation. The analysis is to assess whether SMIs have been less suited to serve these objectives than larger establishments in their given economic environment, and whether SMIs could make a more important contribution in a different policy framework. The issue considered in this chapter concerns the key question whether SMIs can use scarce resources efficiently, i.e. enhance growth, as well as provide remunerative jobs to reduce employment and poverty problems. SMIs can only be agents of economic development if they are able to serve both objectives simultaneously.

The analysis is based on plant size characteristics such as capital intensities which indicate employment effects of changes in the plant size structure, and labor productivities as well as wage rates which provide a yardstick for income generation. The efficiency of factor use in SMIs depends on both capital and labor inputs compared to capital and labor inputs in other establishments.

The summary of plant size characteristics of ASEAN countries provided in Table 3-1 shows a fairly uniform change in capital intensity when plant size is changed [1]. Capital intensity increases with plant size, although this change in factor proportions is less marked in Malaysia and Singapore than in the Philippines and Thailand. As well, capital requirements per unit of output tend to increase with plant size in all countries except Thailand.

Contrary to this pattern, there is a much wider variation of labor input coefficients, i.e. labor productivities, between establishments of different size in ASEAN countries. Labor productivities are excep-

25

Table 3-1: ASEAN Countries - Capital Intensities and Factor Input Coefficients for Total Manufacturing by Establishment Size, Indices[a]

Country[b]	All establish-ments	Establishments with 10+ persons engaged				Ratios	
		P e r s o n s e n g a g e d				(1 - 9)	(10-49)
	1 - 9	10-49	50-99	100-199	200 +	(200+)	(200+)

Capital intensities (fixed assets/persons engaged)

Malaysia	0.28	0.55	0.89	1.15	1.20	0.23	0.46
Philippines	0.14	0.50	0.84	1.15	1.67	0.08	0.30
Singapore	-	0.58	0.82	0.94	1.18	-	0.49
Thailand[e]	0.71	0.56	0.63	0.76	1.65	0.43	0.34

Capital input coefficients (fixed assets/value added)

Malaysia	0.71	0.83	0.88	1.00	1.08	0.66	0.77
Philippines	0.80	0.82	0.80	0.92	1.05	0.76	0.78
Singapore	-	0.80	1.02	1.00	1.04	-	0.77
Thailand[e]	1.71	1.06	0.74	0.80	1.13	1.51	0.94

Labor input coefficients (persons engaged/value added)

Indonesia	4.60	2.43	1.28	0.91[c]	0.64[d]	7.19	3.80
Malaysia	2.53	1.50	0.98	0.87	0.90	2.81	1.67
Philippines	5.54	1.62	0.95	0.80	0.64	8.66	2.53
Singapore	-	1.73	1.22	1.06	0.85	-	2.04
Thailand	2.40	1.88	1.18	1.06	0.68	3.53	2.76
Japan	1.99	1.44	1.29	1.10	0.77	2.58	1.87
USA	1.09	1.19	1.20	1.13	0.91	1.20	1.31

[a]Figure for respective plant size group/figure for all establishments or for establishments with 10+ persons engaged. See footnote 2 in Ch.2.- [b]Indonesia (1974/75),Malaysia (1973), Philippines (1975), Singapore (1978), Thailand (1976), Japan (1973), USA (1972). - [c]100-499. - [d]500+. - [e]Sample survey (1049 observations).

Source: United Nations (UN) (1979), The 1973 World Programme of Industrial Statistics, Summary of Data from Selected Countries. New York; Biro Pusat Statistik (BPS) (Indonesia), 1974/75 Industrial Census. Jakarta, 1976-1978; Department of Statistics (Malaysia) (1973); National Census and Statistics Office (NCSO) (1975), Summary Statistics of Manufacturing Establishments, Manila, unpublished; Department of Statistics (Singapore) (1979); Tambunlertchai, Loohawenchit (1980).

tionally low in Indonesian and Philippine CIs but exceptionally high in their LIs. This is in clear contrast to labor productivity in mature western economies such as the USA, where labor productivity varies little with changes in plant size. The manufacturing sector of Japan is, however, characterized by a dualistic structure, with labor productivity differing with establishment size, similar to the situation observed in Malaysia and Singapore.

Differences in labor productivity between establishments can be due to a number of factors. There may be factor substitution within a given technology [2] between plant sizes; establishments of different sizes may use different technologies (technological heterogeneity); or, there may be differences in the efficiency of factor use. Factor substitution alone is hardly sufficient to explain the great variations in labor productivity observed in ASEAN countries; the observed variation must be the cumulative result of factor substitution and technological heterogeneity, which we shall call structural heterogeneity. Structural heterogeneity may imply inefficient factor use in establishments of a certain size class. The importance of these factors in ASEAN countries will be evaluated in the subsequent sections.

(a)   Indonesia, Thailand, and the Philippines

Among ASEAN countries, the manufacturing sector of Indonesia is the most heterogeneous in terms of establishment characteristics. The fact that only 4.5 per cent of workers in establishments with up to four persons engaged are paid employees clearly shows the highly informal character of these very small establishments (Table 3-2); these are generally either household industries or small workshops depending on family labor. In the somewhat larger CIs (five to nine persons engaged), about three quarters of all workers are paid employees, and this share steadily increases with plant size (Table 3-2). Many CIs do not operate continuously during the whole year, as is common among MIs and LIs; the number of man-days per worker increases from a low 110 days per year in establishments with one to four persons engaged to 248 days per year in establishments with 500 or more persons engaged. In 1974/75, at the lower end of the size spectrum, value added per man-day was US-$ 0.46 as opposed to US-$ 9.28 in very large establishments. In establishments with 5-19 persons engaged, it was only around US-$ 2.32 per day. Differences in wage rates are, however, much smaller than differences in labor productivity. Under neoclassical assumptions this would imply a value for the elasticity of factor substitution far

Table 3-2: Indonesia - Characteristics of Manufacturing Establishments
            by Size, 1974/75

Size (persons engaged)	Days worked[a]	Wage employ- ment[b]	Labor Productivity[d]		Wages paid per employee
			Persons engaged	Man-day	
		(per cent)		(Rp. 1000)	
1 - 4	110	4.5	–	21.2	0.19	56.6
5 - 9	145	72.2	0.4	134.6	0.93	54.8
10 - 14	192	86.2	1.6	176.5	0.92	63.3
15 - 19	215	91.0	2.8	205.2	0.95	75.3
20 - 49	226	95.8	51.0	311.8	1.38	81.9
50 - 74	229	98.4	68.2	371.1	1.62	96.9
75 - 99	232	99.1		646.4	2.79	114.2
100 - 499	235	99.8	82.8	679.5	2.89	140.2
500+	248	100.0	100.0	955.7	3.85	171.8
Total	132	22.7	8.4	124.0	0.94	106.6

[a]Man-days per person engaged. - [b]Share of paid employees in total no.
of persons engaged. - [c]Share of establishments with power-driven machinery. -[d]Value added per person engaged, ... per man-day.

Source: Biro Pusat Statistik (BPS) (Indonesia), 1974/75 Industrial
        Census. Jakarta, 1976-1978.

above unity. A number of empirical investigations [3]
have shown, however, that sufficiently homogenous technologies are characterized by much smaller elasticities
of factor substitution and that an elasticity of factor
substitution greater than unity can be regarded as an
indication of the existence of technological heterogeneity.

   This conclusion is supported by information about
the share of establishments with power-driven machinery. Establishments with up to 19 persons engaged use
hardly any such equipment, and in the group of establishments employing 20-49 persons, only half the establishments have installed some power-driven machinery
(Table 3-2). The use of traditional techniques of
production is not necessarily inefficient under the
conditions of the Indonesian economy, but there is some
indication that intermediate and even modern techniques are generally superior to traditional techniques. Hill (1979) has shown this for the case of the
weaving industry in Indonesia, and similar cases in
other countries are discussed in Morawetz (1974, p.
500). A more rigorous analysis of the Indonesian case
is not possible, since necessary data on capital inputs
are not available.

Size-specific structural heterogeneity is hardly less pronounced in the Philippines than in Indonesia. A common feature in both countries is the existence of predominantly traditional CIs on the one hand and highly capital-intensive LIs on the other (Table 3-3). In the Philippines, the contribution of SIs to the generation of private income (wages and salaries) is much higher than that of CIs, and SIs have a higher degree of organization and operate almost continuously during the year, unlike CIs. However, SIs are relatively more labor-intensive than MIs and much more so than LIs (Table 3-3). Capital productivity in SIs is about the same as in MIs, but labor productivity is much lower. This observation raises doubts about the relative efficiency of SIs, a question that will be discussed in detail in the subsequent section.

The degree to which capital intensities, labor productivities and average annual wages in establishments of different size have been changing in the Philippines can be seen from Table 3-4. This evidence for the 1968/1974 period strengthens the earlier hypothesis that the persistence of very small establishments in terms of employment shares must be regarded as a consequence of the unresolved employment problem. Easy entry into informal traditional sectors combined with a lack of financial resources of new entrepreneurs has resulted in decreasing capital intensities, almost stagnant labor productivities, and a very slow growth of wage rates in nominal terms in establishments with 5-19 persons engaged. The latter implies a steady decline of wages in real terms during this period.

Simultaneously, MIs and LIs with more than 200 persons engaged have experienced above-average growth rates in their capital intensities, labor productivities and wage rates. This suggests that industrial policies favored modern, capital-intensive production techniques in large-scale establishments, thus contributing to a low degree of labor absorption within LIs.

For Thailand, the 1976 sample survey [4] provides some useful insights into the characteristics of larger establishments (Table 3-5). As expected, capital intensity increases with plant size, but only establishments with 200 and more persons engaged are more capital-intensive than any of the groups of smaller establishments. This may have been the result of policies favoring large-scale capital-intensive industries. Capital productivity is rather low in these large establishments, while labor productivity is relatively high. Establishments with fewer than 50 persons engaged appear to be inefficient in the sense that they use more labor as well as more capital per unit of value added than larger establishments.

Table 3-3: Philippines - Characteristics of Manufacturing Establishments[a] by Size, 1975

Size (persons engaged)	Days worked[b]	Capital productivity[c]	Labor productivity[d]		Capital intensity[e]		Wages[f] (₱ 1000) per	
			Person engaged	Man-day	Person engaged	Man-day	paid employee	100-man-days
1 – 9	134	0.98	3.7	2.8	3.8	2.9	1.7	1.3
10 – 49	224	0.95	12.8	5.7	13.4	6.0	3.7	1.6
50 – 99	226	0.97	21.7	9.6	22.4	9.9	4.8	2.1
100 – 199	239	0.85	26.1	10.9	30.6	12.8	5.5	2.3
200 +	227	0.74	32.6	14.4	44.3	19.6	5.9	2.6
Total	201	0.78	20.8	10.3	26.5	13.1	5.0	2.5

[a]Without petroleum refineries and basic metal industries. - [b]Man-days per person engaged. - [c]Value added/fixed assets. - [d]Value added (₱ 1000) per person engaged, ... per 100 man-days. - [e]Fixed assets (₱ 1000) per person engaged, ... per 100 man-days. - [f]Assuming 1.8 unpaid workers per establishment.

Source: National Census and Statistics Office (NCSO) (1975), Summary Statistics of Manufacturing Establishments, Manila, unpublished.

Table 3-4: Philippines - Labor Productivity, Capital
Intensity and Average Wages in Manufacturing
Establishments by Size, 1968-1974

Size (persons engaged)	1968	1970	1973	1974	GR [a] 1974 / 68
Value added (₱ 1000) per person engaged					
5 - 19	3.7	4.3	4.3	4.5	3.5
20 - 49	7.1	8.3	12.1	15.2	13.5
50 - 99	8.4	12.4	15.6	21.6	17.1
100 - 199	13.7	18.2	22.2	29.0	13.3
200+	14.6	19.8	26.8	38.5	17.5
T o t a l	11.4	15.5	20.9	29.4	17.1
Fixed assets (₱ 1000) per person engaged					
5 - 19	5.4	4.5	3.8	4.7	-2.3
20 - 49	6.6	8.9	8.6	8.7	4.7
50 - 99	8.4	10.5	15.7	15.2	10.4
100 - 199	14.9	15.2	18.4	19.7	4.8
200+	13.2	18.2	26.3	25.8	11.8
T o t a l	11.0	14.2	19.9	19.1	9.6
Average annual wages (₱ 1000) per person engaged					
5 - 19	1.3	1.5	1.6	1.6	3.5
20 - 49	2.2	2.6	3.1	3.3	7.0
50 - 99	2.6	3.1	3.6	4.1	7.9
100 - 199	3.0	3.6	4.1	4.7	7.8
200+	3.2	3.8	4.6	5.4	9.1
T o t a l	2.7	3.2	3.9	4.5	8.9

[a] Average annual growth rates.

Source: University of the Philippines Institute for Small-
Scale Industries (UPISSI) (1977), A Study on
Philippine Small- and Medium-Scale Industries,
Phase I. Quezon City, November.

Table 3-5:   Thailand - Characteristics of Manufacturing
Establishments by Size, 1976

Size (persons engaged)	Capital productivity[a]	Labor productivity[b]	Capital intensity[c]	Monthly wages (฿) per person engaged
			(฿ 1000)	
1 - 9	0.28	22.5	79.8	1074
10 - 49	0.46	29.1	63.2	1059
50 - 99	0.66	46.6	70.5	1275
100 - 199	0.61	51.9	85.4	1309
200+	0.43	80.1	185.3	1282
T o t a l	0.48	54.1	111.8	1218

[a] Value added/fixed assets. - [b] Value added per person engaged. -
[c] Fixed assets per person engaged.

Source: Tambunlertchai, Loohawenchit (1980, pp. 34, 41, 44).

(b)   Malaysia and Singapore

Compared with both Indonesia and the Philippines,
the Malaysian manufacturing sector is far less heterogeneous with respect to its basic structural characteristics. Very small establishments, especially those
with fewer than ten persons engaged, show a significantly higher degree of formal organization; they
operate on about twice as many days per year as establishments of similar size in Indonesia (Tables 3-2 and
3-6). Capital intensity is increasing, with plant sizes
of up to 200-249 persons engaged. In contrast with
Indonesia and the Philippines, very large establishments (500 and more persons engaged) are only about as
capital-intensive as MIs in Malaysia. This appears to
be due to foreign direct investment in labor-intensive
electronics and textiles industries [5]. Average wage
rates in these very large establishments are relatively
low as a large number of unskilled workers is employed.
Such development was even more pronounced in
Singapore, where capital intensity is greatest in
establishments with 200-299 persons employed (Table
3-7). In Singapore, however, the characteristics of
establishment vary less directly with plant size than
in Malaysia. This may be due to highly competitive

Table 3-6: Malaysia - Characteristics of Manufacturing Establishments by Size, 1973

Size (persons engaged)	Days worked[a]	Wage employment[b] (per cent)	Capital productivity[c]	Labor productivity[d] Person engaged[f]	Labor productivity[d] Man-day[g]	Capital intensity[e] Person engaged[f]	Capital intensity[e] Man-day[g]	Wages (M$) per paid employee	Wages (M$) per paid man-day
1 - 4	274	37.2	1.35	2.59	0.95	1.92	0.70	1 372	5.01
5 - 9	283	64.2	1.48	3.65	1.29	2.46	0.87	1 614	5.70
10 - 19	286	84.5	1.40	4.58	1.60	3.28	1.15	1 771	6.19
20 - 29	291	92.9	1.49	5.95	2.04	4.00	1.37	1 835	6.31
30 - 49	287	95.8	1.03	6.41	2.23	6.24	2.17	2 018	7.03
50 - 99	287	98.7	1.14	8.64	3.01	7.57	2.64	2 319	8.08
100 - 199	290	99.7	1.00	9.74	3.36	9.70	3.34	2 375	8.19
200 - 499	298	100.0	0.80	9.95	3.34	12.37	4.15	2 330	7.82
500 - 999	298	100.0	0.90	7.75	2.60	8.59	2.88	2 177	7.31
1000 +	307	100.0	1.33	9.69	3.16	7.28	2.37	1 972	6.42
Total	281	93.6	1.01	7.96	2.83	7.84	2.79	2 146	7.64

[a]Average no. of days on which establishments were working. - [b]Share of paid employees in total no. of persons engaged. - [c]Value added/fixed assets. - [d]Value added (M$ 1000) per person engaged, ... per 100 man-days. - [e]Fixed assets (M$ 1000) per person engaged, ... per 100 man-days. - [f]Part-time workers have a weight of 0.5. - [g]Man-days = persons engaged x days worked.

Source: Department of Statistics (Malaysia) (1973).

Table 3-7:   Singapore - Characteristics of Manufacturing
              Establishments by Size, 1978

Size (persons engaged)	Capital productivity[a]	Labor productivity[b]	Capital intensity[c]	Wages per person engaged
			(S$ 1000)	
5 - 9	-	8.86	-	3.97
10 - 19	1.18	15.68	13.25	5.17
20 - 29	0.76	13.04	17.09	7.02
30 - 39	0.81	15.09	18.66	6.41
40 - 49	0.84	17.37	20.76	6.74
50 - 59	0.76	16.25	21.37	6.78
60 - 69	0.87	17.52	20.08	6.96
70 - 79	0.63	19.40	30.93	7.36
80 - 89	0.75	15.08	21.39	6.91
90 - 99	0.66	16.99	25.55	6.61
100 - 149	0.80	21.03	26.26	7.28
150 - 199	0.65	18.53	28.69	7.06
200 - 299	0.51	26.55	52.16	7.58
300 - 499	0.69	26.53	38.55	7.68
500 - 749	0.85	18.00	21.16	6.66
750 - 999	0.82	18.90	23.08	6.75
1000+	0.73	26.13	36.03	7.60
T o t a l	0.73	21.18	29.02	7.07

[a] Value added/fixed assets. - [b] Value added per person engaged. -
[c] Fixed assets per person engaged.

Source: Department of Statistics (Singapore, 1978).

factor and product markets, that do not provide advantages for any particular establishment size group.

As has already been shown above, the industrial
structure of Malaysia and Singapore has changed significantly since the late 1960s, when the inflow of foreign direct investment contributed to an absorption of
surplus labor, higher wage rates and an absolute
decline of traditional industries. This development
also had significant positive impact on the productivity of SIs and MIs as is clearly reflected in Tables
3-8 and 3-9. In the 1960s, when import substitution was
still the predominant feature of industrialization in
Malaysia, labor productivity rose fastest in LIs
(1963-1968; Table 3-8). This suggests that import
substitution policies have favored the adoption of
capital-intensive techniques of production almost exclusively for LIs. Subsequently, when industrialization
policies changed in the late 1960s and export expansion
and the attraction of foreign direct investment became
important, labor productivity declined in LIs, but rose
sharply in SIs and MIs (1968-1973; Table 3-8).

In Singapore, import substitution never was a
policy objective. In the period from 1963 to 1968, very
small and very large establishments both experienced a
decline in labor productivity (Table 3-9). For the very
small establishments, this presumably was due to the
persistent employment problem, while for the very large
establishments, declining labor productivity reflects
structural adjustment in favor of a large-scale labor-
intensive export sector. Industrial labor absorption
gained momentum after 1968 when the inflow of foreign
direct investment was enhanced. The tightening of the
labor market forced small establishments to rapidly
increase their labor productivity in order to remain
competitive in factor markets. After 1973, when full
employment was achieved, growth of labor productivity
continued to be high in all size groups of establishments. This suggests that in the 1973/78 period of
consolidation and reorientation, there was little bias
in the economic environment favoring specific size
groups of industrial establishments.

Part 2: Employment and Production Effects
        in Industrial Subsectors

Policy makers are interested in the SMI sector
mainly because this sector is expected to generate
additional employment opportunities and to be an efficient user of resources. The analysis of SMIs in individual industries can provide valuable clues with
respect to the conditions and the type of industries
for which such expectations may be justified.

Table 3-8: Malaysia - Average Annual Growth Rates of Labor Productivity in Manufacturing Establishments of Different Size, 1963-1973, per cent

Size (paid full-time employees)	Value added per person engaged	Value added per paid employee		
	1963-1973	1963-1968	1968-1973	1963-1973
0 - 9	2.10	1.41	2.79	2.10
5 - 19	4.21	3.56	7.42	5.47
20 - 49	5.08	3.70	6.48	5.08
50 - 99	5.52	2.80	8.82	5.51
100 - 199	4.77	11.18	-1.23	4.79
200 - 499	3.70	3.71	3.72	3.71
500+	3.61	8.77	-1.31	3.61
T o t a l	6.53	6.88	4.45	5.66

Source: See Table 3-9.

Table 3-9: Singapore - Average Annual Growth Rates of Labor Productivity in Manufacturing Establishments of Different Size, 1963-1978, per cent

Size (persons engaged)	Value added per person engaged			
	1963-1968	1968-1973	1973-1978	1963-1978
5 - 9	-0.4	10.4	11.2	6.9
10 - 29	4.6	14.9	7.2	8.8
30 - 49	5.5	10.8	11.4	9.2
50 - 99	4.3	2.3	7.9	4.8
100 - 299	5.9	7.3	10.2	7.8
300+	-3.2	7.8	11.0	5.3
T o t a l	3.6	10.0	10.7	8.1

Source: Department of Statistics (Malaysia, 1963, 1968, 1973); University of the Philippines Institute for Small-Scale Industries (UPISSI), A Study on Philippine Small- and Medium-Scale Industries, Phase I. Quezon City, November 1977 and unpublished material; Department of Statistics (Singapore, 1963, 1968, 1973, 1978).

Table 3-10: Selected ASEAN Countries - Capital Intensities of Manufacturing Industries by Size Groups (Indices)[a,b]

Industry (ISIC) Country[c]		All establishments CI	Establishments with 10+ persons engaged				Total industries[d] (indices)
		CI	SI	MI	LI 1	LI 2	
Food (311-2)	MAL	0.35	0.68	1.11	1.43	1.03	1.17
	PHI	0.19	0.42	0.90	0.95	1.20	1.11
	SIN	-	0.50	1.41	0.88	1.33	1.91
Beverages (313)	MAL	0.16	0.22	0.39	1.09	2.01	1.73
	PHI	0.06	0.61	1.04	1.90	0.98	0.58
	SIN	-	-	-	-	-	1.76
Tobacco (314)	MAL	0.26	0.17	0.18	0.14	2.28	0.60
	PHI	-	0.93	0.42	1.48	1.00	0.50
	SIN	-	-	-	-	-	1.75
Textiles (321)	MAL	0.28	0.45	0.26	0.49	1.13	1.29
	PHI	0.04	0.30	0.91	0.40	1.15	1.09
	SIN	-	0.40	1.23	0.92	1.03	1.16
Clothing (322)	MAL	1.11	0.86	0.89	1.33	1.03	0.23
	PHI	0.72	1.30	1.59	1.94	0.75	0.11
	SIN	-	0.55	0.82	0.60	1.14	0.22
Leather and l. products (323)	MAL	0.58	1.00	1.13	0.67	-	0.34
	PHI	0.19	0.70	0.54	1.41	-	0.46
	SIN	-	0.98	1.03	-	-	0.40
Footwear (324)	MAL	0.53	0.39	0.68	1.41	1.84	0.36
	PHI	0.59	0.43	1.04	2.31	-	0.15
	SIN	-	1.17		0.95		0.40
Wood and cork products (331)	MAL	0.41	0.62	0.86	0.94	1.36	0.93
	PHI	0.19	0.41	1.08	0.51	1.22	0.81
	SIN	-	0.31	0.65	1.14	1.38	1.09
Furniture (332)	MAL	0.76	0.84	0.73	1.53	-	0.33
	PHI	0.61	0.77	2.14	1.22	0.69	0.17
	SIN	-	0.54	0.45	1.43		0.52
Paper and p. products (341)	MAL	0.32	0.51	1.26	1.52	0.86	0.92
	PHI	0.06	0.11	0.11	1.83	1.08	4.36
	SIN	-	0.52	0.60	1.64	-	1.06
Printing and publishing (342)	MAL	0.66	0.75	0.92	1.11	1.29	0.79
	PHI	0.50	0.70	1.12	1.05	1.80	0.51
	SIN	-	0.66	0.94	1.59	1.27	0.99
Industrial chemicals (351)	MAL	0.28	0.74	1.39	1.01	1.02	7.55
	PHI	0.54	0.72	0.39	0.69	1.38	4.91
	SIN	-	-	-	-	-	5.25
Other chemicals (352)	MAL	0.33	0.62	1.34	0.84	1.16	0.86
	PHI	0.31	0.60	1.06	1.00	1.06	0.92
	SIN	-	0.18	0.72	1.57		1.65
Rubber products (355)	MAL	0.43	0.96	1.26	1.10	0.93	0.88
	PHI	0.21	0.30	0.37	0.45	1.38	1.34
	SIN	-	-	-	-	-	1.96
Plastic products (356)	MAL	0.74	0.98	1.26	1.27	0.80	0.92
	PHI	0.45	1.06	1.30	0.81	0.96	0.95
	SIN	-	1.06	1.07	0.89		1.09
Pottery, china, earthenware (361)	MAL	0.10	0.18	-	1.27	1.77	0.86
	PHI	0.03	0.31	-	-	1.08	1.24
	SIN	-	-	-	-	-	1.54
Glass and gl. products (362)	MAL	0.11	0.17	-	-	1.14	3.34
	PHI	0.20	0.22	-	-	1.04	1.82
	SIN	-	-	-	-	-	1.57

continued

Table 3-10   (Cont.)

Industry (ISIC) Country[c]		All establishments CI	Establishments with 10+ persons engaged				Total industries[d] (indices)
			SI	MI	LI 1	LI 2	
Other non-metallic mineral products (369)	MAL	0.18	0.22	0.27	0.63	2.26	2.19
	PHI	0.03	0.05	0.12	0.31	1.66	6.85
	SIN	-		1.36		0.81	1.70
Metal products (381)	MAL	0.36	0.46	0.65	1.27	1.52	1.01
	PHI	0.28	0.65	0.72	1.07	1.25	0.52
	SIN	-	0.69	1.26	1.07	1.08	1.26
Non-electrical machinery (382)	MAL	0.84	0.62	0.88	0.85	2.14	0.59
	PHI	0.72	0.78	0.73	1.10	1.53	0.54
	SIN	-	0.42	0.94	3.35	0.89	1.44
Electrical machinery (383)	MAL	1.49	1.60	1.61	2.28	0.85	0.53
	PHI	0.42	0.59	0.62	1.27	0.96	0.71
	SIN	-	1.52	1.84	1.68	0.95	0.47
Transport equipment (384)	MAL	0.45	0.58	1.11	1.31	1.01	0.61
	PHI	0.31	0.40	0.46	1.45	1.30	0.75
	SIN	-	0.50	0.72	0.66	1.07	1.36
Professional goods, etc.(385)	MAL	0.95	0.81	1.23	-	0.99	0.61
	PHI	2.30	0.89	0.70	2.34	0.47	0.43
	SIN	-		0.24		1.08	1.58
Other manufacturing (390)	MAL	0.60	0.79	1.03	1.01	1.48	0.52
	PHI	0.39	0.79	1.54	1.35	-	0.22
	SIN	-	1.03	1.31		0.91	0.41

[a]For definition of size groups see Ch. 1.2. LI 1: 100-199 persons engaged, LI 2: 200+ persons engaged. - [b]Indices are calculated as fixed assets per person engaged in respective size group/ fixed assets per person engaged in total industry or in establishments with 10+ persons engaged. Indices for CIs refer to all establishments, indices for the other size groups only refer to establishments with 10+ persons engaged. See footnote 2 in Ch.2.- [c]Malaysia (1973), Philippines (1975), Singapore (1973). - [d]Indices are calculated as capital intensity of respective industry/capital intensity of total manufacturing in resp. country.

Source: United Nations (UN) (1979), The 1973 World Programme of Industrial Statistics, Summary of Data from Selected Countries. New York; Biro Pusat Statistik (BPS) (Indonesia), 1974/75 Industrial Census. Jakarta, 1976-1978; Department of Statistics (Malaysia) (1973); National Census and Statistics Office (NCSO) (1975), Summary Statistics of Manufacturing Establishments, Manila, unpublished; Department of Statistics (Singapore) (1979); Tambunlertchai, Loohawenchit (1980).

Capital intensities of individual industries provide an indication of the employment effect of SMIs in ASEAN countries. For the countries in Table 3-10, it can be observed that in the majority of industries, capital intensity increases with plant size. This finding corresponds to the general picture for total manufacturing, discussed in the preceding section. However, there are a number of exceptions to this rule in the cases of Singapore, Malaysia and the Philippines.

In a number of industries, MIs in particular use more fixed assets per employee than LIs. Establishments with 200 and more persons engaged (LI2) often are less capital-intensive than establishments with 100-199 persons employed (LI1). SIs and CIs on the other hand, are generally the most labor-intensive establishments in any given industry [6]. These observations suggest that the link between capital intensity and plant size becomes less close once industrial establishments exceeded a certain size limit. This size limit seems to differ among industries and countries. A comparison between countries (Table 3-11) reveals that the critical level is lower in Singapore than in Malaysia and the Philippines [7]. These findings correspond to the differences in capital intensity among countries observed earlier with respect to total manufacturing. The data provide further evidence to support the hypothesis that technological heterogeneity among establishments of different size groups are less pronounced where competitive product markets, access to credit and availability of technology support an efficient division of labor between establishments of different sizes.

A rough idea of how the efficiency of factor use varies among establishments of different size can be developed by comparing factor input coefficients [8]. As can be observed in Table 3-12, in Malaysia and the Philippines in most industries, CIs are using more fixed capital to produce one unit of value added than at least one of the other size groups [9]. As CIs are the most labor-intensive group in almost all industries, they seem to be clearly inferior to larger establishments in the sense that they use more of both factors of production per unit of value added. This finding should not be overemphasized, however, since the data pertaining to CIs are likely to be incomplete in coverage. A thorough analysis of the relative efficiency of CIs would require additional field research, going beyond the scope of this study.

40

Table 3-11: No. of Industries by Capital Intensity Rank of Size Groups[a]

Country	Size Group	Rank 5	4	3	2	1
MAL	CI	16	6	–	2	–
	SI	4	14	6	–	–
	MI	2	1	8	7	4
	LI1	1	1	4	10	6
	LI2	1	2	4	3	12
PHI	CI	20	2	–	1	–
	SI	1	15	6	2	–
	MI	1	4	8	6	3
	LI1	–	1	6	9	6
	LI2	1	2	2	4	12
SIN[b]	SI	–	13	2	2	2
	MI	–	3	7	4	7
	LI1	–	2	9	8	5
	LI2	–	3	4	9	6

[a]Largest number of industries is underlined. - [b]Multiple entries in case of inadequate disaggregation by plant size.

Source: United Nations (UN) (1979), The 1973 World Programme of Industrial Statistics, Summary of Data from Selected Countries. New York; Biro Pusat Statistik (BPS) (Indonesia), 1974/75 Industrial Census. Jakarta, 1976-1978; Department of Statistics (Malaysia) (1973); National Census and Statistics Office (NCSO) (1975), Summary Statistics of Manufacturing Establishments, Manila, unpublished; Department of Statistics (Singapore) (1979); Tambunlertchai, Loohawenchit (1980).

Table 3-12: ASEAN Countries[a] - Capital and Labor Input Coefficients of Manufacturing Industries by Size Groups (Indices)[b,c]

ISIC	Country[d]	Fixed assets/value added					Persons engaged/value added				
		All establishments	Establishments with 10+ persons engaged				All establishments	Establishments with 10+ persons engaged			
		CI	SI	MI	LI 1	LI 2	CI	SI	MI	LI 1	LI 2
311-2	IND	-	-	-	-	-	3.06	2.31	0.76	0.72	0.76
	MAL	0.94	0.95	0.72	0.99	1.21	2.66	1.39	0.65	0.69	1.17
	PHI	1.37	1.79	1.77	1.09	0.92	7.25	4.23	1.98	1.16	0.77
	SIN	-	0.89	0.97	1.00	1.10	-	1.76	0.68	1.13	0.83
313	IND	-	-	-	-	-	18.53	9.61	2.09	0.77	0.36
	MAL	1.16	1.07	0.84	0.69	1.38	7.41	4.90	2.16	0.63	0.67
	PHI	0.79	0.88	1.36	3.18	0.94	14.18	1.44	1.30	1.66	0.96
	SIN	-	-	-	-	-	-	-	-	-	-
314	IND	-	-	-	-	-	9.53	56.64	5.41	1.47	0.75
	MAL	2.72	1.83	1.51	1.13	0.96	10.28	11.11	8.60	8.19	0.42
	PHI	-	1.09	0.35	0.47	1.11	-	1.18	0.85	0.32	1.10
	SIN	-	-	-	-	-	-	-	-	-	-
321	IND	-	-	-	-	-	8.49	1.05	4.75	1.09	0.70
	MAL	0.55	0.58	0.46	0.50	1.08	1.94	1.29	1.77	1.02	0.96
	PHI	0.24	0.30	0.67	0.53	1.15	5.41	1.00	0.73	1.31	1.00
	SIN	-	0.74	1.37	0.73	1.02	-	1.83	1.12	0.79	0.99
322	IND	-	-	-	-	-	1.29	0.90	1.31	1.50	-
	MAL	1.18	0.99	0.89	0.61	1.12	1.06	1.14	1.00	0.46	1.09
	PHI	1.15	1.33	1.04	1.45	0.82	1.60	1.03	0.65	0.75	1.10
	SIN	-	0.57	0.67	0.46	1.18	-	1.05	0.82	0.76	1.04
323	IND	-	-	-	-	-	2.22	1.27	1.24	0.69	-
	MAL	1.00	1.10	0.80	4.29	-	1.74	1.10	0.71	6.37	-
	PHI	1.26	0.71	0.64	1.31	-	6.80	1.01	1.17	0.93	-
	SIN	-	0.84	1.36	-	-	-	0.86	1.32	-	-
324	IND	-	-	-	-	-	1.42	-0.32	0.68	0.61	0.29
	MAL	0.78	0.52	0.89	1.33	1.29	1.49	1.33	1.30	0.95	0.70
	PHI	0.92	0.55	1.04	1.55	-	1.56	1.27	1.00	0.67	-
	SIN	-	1.30		0.92		-	1.11		0.97	
331	IND	-	-	-	-	-	23.92	1.85	1.19	0.53	0.71
	MAL	0.88	0.71	0.77	0.78	1.51	2.14	1.15	0.89	0.83	1.11
	PHI	0.60	0.47	0.71	0.58	1.24	3.19	1.16	0.66	1.13	1.04
	SIN	-	0.37	0.80	1.32	1.21	-	1.17	1.22	1.16	0.88
332	IND	-	-	-	-	-	3.35	1.27	1.43	0.80	-
	MAL	1.00	0.93	0.87	1.14	-	1.32	1.11	1.19	0.75	-
	PHI	0.78	0.76	1.70	1.13	0.64	1.29	1.07	0.86	1.00	1.01
	SIN	-	0.44	0.60	1.56		-	0.81	1.35	1.09	
341	IND	-	-	-	-	-	5.49	2.67	1.90	1.23	0.78
	MAL	0.56	0.70	1.44	1.32	0.73	1.76	1.38	1.14	0.87	0.85
	PHI	0.31	0.39	0.20	1.03	1.09	5.05	3.42	1.93	0.57	1.01
	SIN	-	1.00	0.85	1.05	-	-	1.91	1.42	0.64	-
342	IND	-	-	-	-	-	2.58	1.62	0.62	0.83	0.89
	MAL	1.02	1.22	1.03	1.24	0.82	1.56	1.63	1.12	1.12	0.63
	PHI	2.03	1.02	2.07	1.36	0.60	4.02	1.46	1.84	1.29	0.33
	SIN	-	0.95	1.29	3.05	0.88	-	1.45	1.38	1.92	0.69
351	IND	-	-	-	-	-	3.26	2.97	1.57	0.99	0.67
	MAL	0.21	0.75	0.88	2.22	0.87	0.77	1.01	0.63	2.21	0.86
	PHI	1.00	1.55	0.57	0.93	0.99	1.85	2.16	1.47	1.35	0.72
	SIN	-	-	-	-	-	-	-	-	-	-
352	IND	-	-	-	-	-	6.92	-3.40	0.73	0.65	0.87
	MAL	1.05	1.05	1.42	1.32	0.83	3.17	1.71	1.06	1.57	0.71
	PHI	1.89	0.71	0.89	0.82	1.13	6.12	1.18	0.84	0.82	1.07
	SIN	-	0.91	0.94	1.06		-	5.12	1.31	0.67	

continued

Table 3-12   (Cont.)

ISIC	Country[d]	All establishments		Establishments with 10+ persons engaged			All establishments		Establishments with 10+ persons engaged		
		CI	SI	MI	LI 1	LI 2	CI	SI	MI	LI 1	LI 2
355	IND	–	–	–	–	–	8.83	1.65	0.92	0.97	0.57
	MAL	1.06	1.06	0.79	0.98	1.07	2.44	1.11	0.63	0.89	1.15
	PHI	0.76	0.73	1.48	1.11	0.99	3.57	2.42	3.96	2.45	0.72
	SIN	–	–	–	–	–	–	–	–	–	–
356	IND	–	–	–	–	–	2.89	1.24	0.90	0.90	–
	MAL	1.30	0.98	0.91	0.91	1.18	1.75	1.00	0.72	0.72	1.47
	PHI	1.03	0.94	1.63	1.36	0.86	2.31	0.90	1.26	1.67	0.89
	SIN	–	1.18	0.81	1.09		–	1.10	0.76	1.23	
361	IND	–	–	–	–	–	1.31	0.60	2.28	4.18	-7.77
	MAL	0.44	0.54	–	0.83	1.67	4.29	3.07	–	0.65	0.94
	PHI	0.60	0.94	–	–	1.01	18.17	2.98	–	–	0.93
	SIN	–	–	–	–	–	–	–	–	–	–
362	IND	–	–	–	–	–	4.00	2.22	4.20	1.97	0.37
	MAL	0.18	0.11	–	–	1.26	1.71	0.62	–	–	1.10
	PHI	0.20	0.17	–	–	1.06	0.99	0.80	–	–	1.01
	SIN	–	–	–	–	–	–	–	–	–	–
369	IND	–	–	–	–	–	1.86	10.80	0.98	1.29	0.13
	MAL	0.61	0.54	0.56	0.74	1.21	3.35	2.52	2.02	1.16	0.51
	PHI	0.23	0.16	0.18	0.29	1.29	8.39	3.33	1.35	0.96	0.78
	SIN	–	1.38		0.80		–	1.01		0.99	
381	IND	–	–	–	–	–	2.83	1.90	0.95	1.33	0.44
	MAL	0.75	0.62	0.66	1.56	1.15	2.09	1.34	1.01	1.23	0.76
	PHI	1.08	0.80	0.82	0.84	1.30	3.87	1.24	1.14	0.79	1.03
	SIN	–	0.88	0.91	0.94	1.22	–	1.28	0.73	0.88	1.12
382	IND	–	–	–	–	–	4.14	2.13	0.41	-2.56	0.34
	MAL	1.43	0.94	0.76	0.87	1.30	1.70	1.52	0.87	1.05	0.61
	PHI	1.05	1.15	0.99	0.54	3.03	1.46	1.48	1.36	0.50	1.98
	SIN	–	0.38	1.03	2.63	1.00	–	0.89	1.09	0.78	1.13
383	IND	–	–	–	–	–	5.05	1.84	2.51	0.75	1.11
	MAL	1.19	2.64	1.78	1.96	0.85	0.80	1.65	1.10	0.82	1.00
	PHI	0.89	1.01	0.87	1.45	0.85	2.09	1.72	1.33	1.14	0.89
	SIN	–	1.73	1.65	1.84	0.94	–	1.14	1.66	1.09	0.99
384	IND	–	–	–	–	–	10.21	3.97	1.54	0.71	0.87
	MAL	1.02	0.98	0.96	0.88	1.05	2.24	1.70	0.86	0.68	1.04
	PHI	1.38	1.34	0.58	1.62	0.92	4.44	3.37	1.27	1.12	0.71
	SIN	–	0.68	1.02	0.58	1.05	–	1.36	1.40	0.88	0.98
385	IND	–	–	–	–	–	1.85	0.85	1.60	2.49	–
	MAL	2.39	1.18	1.39	–	0.96	2.51	1.46	1.13	–	0.97
	PHI	2.32	0.69	0.78	2.15	0.52	1.01	0.78	1.12	0.09	1.11
	SIN	–	0.29		1.06		–	1.22		0.98	
390	IND	–	–	–	–	–	1.76	1.49	1.28	0.60	0.82
	MAL	1.09	0.68	1.52	1.06	1.31	1.81	0.87	1.47	1.05	0.89
	PHI	0.61	0.83	1.84	1.06	–	1.59	1.06	1.21	0.80	–
	SIN	–	0.64	1.06	1.54		–	0.62	0.81	1.82	

[a]Without Thailand. – [b]For definition of size groups see Table 3-10. – [c]Indices are calculated as value for respective size group/value for all establishments (CI) or value for establishments with 10+ persons engaged. See footnote 2 in Chapter 2. – [d]Indonesia (1974/75), Malaysia (1973), Philippines (1975), Singapore (1973).

Source: See Table 3-10.

Table 3-12 shows that there are only a few industries in which the capital input coefficient exclusively increases or decreases with plant size. In the Philippines, but particularly in Malaysia, U-shaped patterns predominate with the minimum of the capital input coefficient being located somewhere in the middle of the size spectrum. However, in some industries SMIs use the least capital per unit of value added. In all countries for which capital investment data are available, this holds true in industries producing wood (331) and metal (381) products, pottery and earthenware (361), and other manufactured products (390). In two of the three countries for which data are available, this is the case with the footwear (324), other chemical products (352), and other nonmetallic mineral products (369) industries. Most of these industries belong to the group of natural resource-based industries. Table 3-12 indicates that LIs in all countries (either LI1 or LI2) have invested the smallest amount of capital per unit of value added in the clothing (322), electrical machinery (383) and printing industries (342). In the cases of clothing and electrical machinery, low capital input coefficients merely reflect labor-intensive production processes while economies of scale could explain high capital productivity in the printing industry.

It is obvious that the input of capital in a manufacturing enterprise involves opportunity costs in the form of output forgone elsewhere in the economy. Under the conditions of a labor-surplus economy, this is less clear for labor as a factor of production. It has been argued, however, that even under labor-surplus conditions labor is far from being available at no cost and that the shadow wage rate may even be substantially higher than the average agricultural wage rate if the cost of labor migration is accounted for [10]. For this reason the production effect of SMIs will also depend on the labor input coefficient (Table 3-12). For Indonesia and the Philippines in particular, it should be noted in most industries that the labor input coefficient varies much more with plant size than the capital input coefficient, even when CIs with their particularly high labor input per unit of value added are excluded from consideration. With the exception of a few industries, in all the countries the smallest labor input coefficient is that of LIs.

Part 3: Measuring Relative Efficiency of Small-,
        Medium-, and Large-Scale Establishments [11]

As is apparent from the preceding discussion, both
labor and capital factor input coefficients must be
considered simultaneously when conclusions with respect
to the relative efficiency of establishments of different size are to be drawn. To determine the relative
efficiency of establishments in different size groups,
the concept of isocost lines is used. Isocost lines
serve two purposes: they allow identification of those
size groups in a manufacturing subsector using more
capital as well as more labor per unit of value added
than other size groups (technical efficiency), and they
distinguish   between   economically   efficient   and
inefficient factor combinations. The basic concept is
demonstrated in Figure 3-1.

Every point in this diagram represents potential
combinations of the capital and labor inputs required
to produce one unit of value added. At point L, the
capital input coefficient (K/V) is higher than in S but
lower than in S^1. The line connecting L and S (or S^1)
is an isocost line, i.e., the location of all factor
combinations with the same per unit costs, provided the
slope of the line is equal to the factor price ratio.
When the slope is positive, as in the case of LS^1, S^1
is technically inefficient since in S^1 both more
capital and labor are used to produce one unit of value
added in S^1 than in L [12].

Figure 3-1:

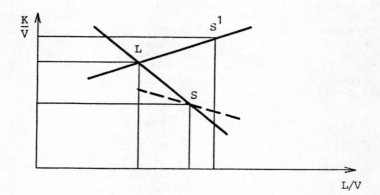

The economic efficiency of either L or S depends
on the factor price ratio. If a small establishment is
much more labor-intensive than a large one but uses
only slightly less capital per unit of value added,
assuming a given price for capital, the small establishment may be efficient if the opportunity costs of
labor are very low (dotted line in the diagram). However, the small establishment may be inefficient if the
shadow wage rate is sufficiently close to the prevailing market wage rate. Economically inefficient size
groups of manufacturing establishments can be identified by comparing the slopes of isocost lines to
relevant factor price ratios.

The numerical values of these slopes for pairwise
combinations of size groups are presented in Table
3-13. Table 3-14 is showing those size groups within
each industrial subsector that are technically efficient. The most important finding emerging from this
analysis is that SMIs are producing as efficiently as
larger establishments in almost all industrial subsectors. There are only two industrial subsectors - printing and publishing (342), electrical machinery (383) -
in which only large establishments are technically
efficient in more than one country. It should be noted,
however, that SIs are efficient in fewer subsectors
than MIs, and that the latter emerge as technically
inefficient only in the production of professional
goods (385) and in other manufacturing (390). Regarding
technical efficiency among SIs, a certain pattern is
discernible in Malaysia and the Philippines but is less
definite in the case of Singapore. In both Malaysia and
the Philippines, SIs are inefficient in "modern" industries such as the nonelectrical (382) and electrical
machinery industries (383) and in the transport equipment industry (384) as well as in "traditional" industries such as clothing (322), food (311-2) and tobacco
(314) products. In Singapore, SIs are technically
efficient in some of these industrial subsectors such
as e.g. clothing (322) and transport equipment (384).
This finding provides an indication that the relative
efficiency of SIs in these sectors may be related to
industrialization policies and/or the general level of
industrialization.

For policy conclusions to be drawn later, Table
3-14 provides a further important information. A comparison of technical efficiency and capital intensity
ranks shows that in many industries, employment and
production effects cannot be simultaneously maximized
simply by changing plant size structure. The promotion
of SMIs may create additional employment at the expense
of output growth in a number of industries.

Technically inefficient establishments of a certain size can be classified as economically inefficient

Table 3-13:   Selected ASEAN Countries — Slopes of Isocost Lines[a]

ISIC	Malaysia			Philippines			Singapore		
	i=L j=S	i=L j=M	i=M j=S	i=L j=S	i=L j=M	i=M j=S	i=L j=S	i=L j=M	i=M j=S
311-2	-4.8	16.0	3.9	11.4	32.6	0.4	-5.3	11.5	-1.8
313	0.2	-2.0	1.4	-4.0	18.4	-55.4	-	-	-
314	0.5	0.4	0.7	5.2	58.1	30.3	-	-	-
321	-16.9	-8.5	-3.0	910.4	45.9	-43.4	-4.5	39.0	-13.1
322	-0.4	-7.4	1.4	-101.8	-1.5	3.7	-34.9	6.6	-1.2
323	2.0	2.1	2.6	-126.1	-43.8	-6.4	-	-	5.6
324	-5.3	-2.6	-42.1	-10.2	-9.5	-11.1	-	-	14.0
331	-22.1	35.7	-0.4	-120.5	27.2	-11.2	-44.6	-18.9	125.7
332	-2.1	-2.2	-2.5	-2.3	-34.8	-25.3	26.1	-25.0	2.0
341	-5.1	14.1	-28.5	-31.8	-95.9	15.1	-0.5	-3.1	3.7
342	2.6	2.4	2.8	3.7	15.6	42.7	-0.4	6.3	-62.1
351	187.3	40.9	-23.7	54.9	-80.4	184.5	-	-	-
352	1.5	20.5	-4.8	-54.6	24.5	-13.0	-0.7	-3.8	-0.2
355	6.0	4.7	4.7	-6.7	5.8	18.5	-	-	-
356	5.3	3.1	2.2	-6.8	68.6	48.6	-9.5	8.3	14.6
369	-6.5	-9.0	-0.7	-90.7	-416.3	-1.4	551.9	-	-
381	-14.1	-45.3	-1.1	-11.2	-20.3	-9.1	-13.7	10.0	-1.0
382	-1.7	-17.5	1.6	4.1	1.2	19.0	125.9	-122.2	58.9
383	12.5	34.3	7.7	0.1	-7.4	8.9	33.4	6.1	-0.9
384	-0.2	3.4	0.1	2.6	-18.7	7.6	-14.2	0.2	160.8
385	2.5	15.1	-3.5	16.6	-40.2	2.8	-64.3	-	-
390	17.9	4.3	7.2	-6.2	13.6	48.6	3.9	2.5	11.9

[a]Definition of size groups: S: 10-49 persons engaged, M: 50-99 persons engaged, L: 100+ persons engaged. $-b[(K/V)_i - (K/V)_j] / [(L/V)_i - (L/V)_j]$, where V = value added and K(L) = capital (labor) input.

Source: United Nations (UN) (1979), The 1973 World Programme of Industrial Statistics, Summary of Data from Selected Countries. New York; Biro Pusat Statistik (BPS) (Indonesia), 1974/75 Industrial Census. Jakarta, 1976-1978; Department of Statistics (Malaysia) (1973); National Census and Statistics Office (NCSO) (1975), Summary Statistics of Manufacturing Establishments, Manila, Philippines; Department of Statistics (Singapore) (1979); Tambunlertchai, Loohawenchit (1980).

Table 3-14: Selected ASEAN Countries - Relative Efficiency of Manufacturing Establishments of Different Size[a]

ISIC	Malaysia		Philippines		Singapore	
	Technically efficient size groups	Capital-intensity rank	Technically efficient size groups	Capital-intensity rank	Technically efficient size groups	Capital-intensity rank
311-2	M	S<M<L	L	S<M<L	S M	S<L<M
313	M L	S<M<L	S L	S<M<L	-	-
314	L	S<M<L	M	M<S<L	-	-
321	S M L	M<S<L	S M	S<M<L	S L	S<L<M
322	M L	S<M<L	M L	L<S<M	S M	S<M<L
323	M	L<S<M	S M L	M<S<L	S	S<M
324	S M L	S<M<L	S M L	S<M<L	M	M<S
331	S M	S<M<L	M L	S<M<L	S L	M<S<L
332	S M L	M<S<L	S M L	S<L<M	S L	M<S<L
341	S L	S<M<L	M L	M<S<L	M L	S<M<L
342	L	S<M<L	L	S<M<L	S L	S<M<L
351	S M	S<L<M	M L	M<S<L	-	-
352	L	S<L<M	S M	S<M<L	S M L	S<M<L
355	M	S<L<M	S L	S<M<L	-	-
356	M	S<L<M	S L	L<S<M	M	L<S<M
369	S M L	S<M<L	S M L	S<M<L	L	L<S
381	S M L	S<M<L	S M L	S<M<L	S M	S<L<M
382	M L	S<M<L	L	S<M<L	S	S<M<L
383	L	L<S<M	M L	S<M<L	L	M<L<S
384	M	S<M<L	M L	S<M<L	S L	S<M<L
385	L	S<L<M	S	M<S<L	S L	S<L
390	S	S<M<L	S L	S<M<L	S	L<S<M

[a]For definition of size groups see Table 3-13.

Source: United Nations (UN) (1979), The 1973 World Programme of Industrial Statistics, Summary of Data from Selected Countries. New York; Biro Pusat Statistik (BPS) (Indonesia), 1974/75 Industrial Census. Jakarta, 1976-1978; Department of Statistics (Malaysia) (1973); National Census and Statistics Office (NCSO) (1975), Summary Statistics of Manufacturing Establishments, Manila, unpublished; Department of Statistics (Singapore) (1979); Tambunlertchai, Loohawenchit (1980).

without reference to factor prices. Depending on factor prices, technically efficient establishments may, however, be economically inefficient. To analyze economic efficiency, the slopes of isocost lines are compared with factor price ratios. Since the opportunity costs of labor and capital prevailing in each country are not known, several factor price ratios were applied in order to assess the sensitivity of the results with respect to changes in factor prices. To obtain a base line estimate for the factor price ratio y, the actual market wage rate (in manufacturing) was divided by an assumed average return on capital of 10 per cent. The highest value for y shown in Table 3-15 corresponds to this ratio, which differs among countries in accordance with different wage rates. The variable y was allowed to decline in three successive steps, reflecting a lower shadow wage rate, higher opportunity costs of capital, or both. In the unlikely case of a shadow wage rate equal to zero, y will equal zero.

The results of the sensitivity analysis are shown in Table 3-15. The asterisks indicate those size groups of establishments that are economically efficient at the various factor price ratios. In all industrial subsectors, there is only one efficient size group for a given price ratio, but efficiency may shift from larger to smaller establishments when y declines, as in textiles (321). However, Table 3-15 reveals that the relative economic efficiency of small-, medium- and large-scale establishments is generally stable with respect to changes in the wage-rental ratio, except for the extreme case of y = 0.

SMIs are economically more efficient than large enterprises in approximately half of all the industrial subsectors in the countries of the sample. Within the SMI sector, there are, however, substantial differences among countries with respect to the relative economic efficiency of small-scale and medium-scale establishments. Assuming the highest wage-rental ratio, which approximately reflects the market price ratio, SIs are efficient in only industrial chemicals (351) and other manufacturing (390) in Malaysia and leather products (323), plastic products (356) and professional instruments (385) in the Philippines. This pattern changes little when the shadow wage rate of labor is assumed to be substantially below the market rate, as in the case of y equal to 10 or 20. Only when a shadow wage rate equal to zero is assumed do SIs become the most efficient size group in a considerably larger number of industries (seven in Malaysia and eleven in the Philippines). Since there is general agreement that the opportunity costs of labor are not adequately reflected by a shadow wage rate of zero, this alternative is omitted from the following considerations.

Table 3-15: Selected ASEAN Countries - Relative Economic Efficiency of Manufacturing Establishments of Different Size; Sensitivity Analysis[a]

#: Size group is economically efficient at factor price ratio y[b]

Country/size-group sub-columns — Malaysia: S, M, L at y = 0, 5, 10, 20; Philippines: S, M, L at y = 0, 10, 20, 50; Singapore: S, M, L at y = 0, 10, 20, 40.

ISIC	Mal S 0	5	10	20	Mal M 0	5	10	20	Mal L 0	5	10	20	Phil S 0	10	20	50	Phil M 0	10	20	50	Phil L 0	10	20	50	Sing S 0	10	20	40	Sing M 0	10	20	40	Sing L 0	10	20	40
311-2					#	#	#	#													#	#	#	#	#					#	#	#				
313					#					#	#	#	#									#	#	#					-				-			
314									#	#	#	#					#	#	#	#					-				-				-			
321	#	#			#							#	#	#	#									#	#									#	#	#
322					#						#	#						#	#	#	#				#					#	#	#				
323					#	#	#	#					#					#	#	#					#	#	#	#						-		
324	#	#									#	#	#	#									#	#	#	#	#	#						-		
331	#									#	#	#	#	#									#	#	#	#	#	#								
332					#					#	#	#	#						#	#				#	#	#	#	#								
341	#										#	#	#	#	#	#									#									#	#	#
342									#	#	#	#									#	#	#	#	#									#	#	#
351	#	#	#	#									#	#	#	#		#	#	#					-				-				-			
352									#	#	#	#	#					#	#	#					#									#	#	#
355					#	#	#	#					#									#	#	#									-			
356					#	#	#	#										#	#	#	#								#	#	#	#				
369	#				#						#	#	#					#	#	#									-				#	#	#	#
381	#					#	#	#					#					#	#					#	#					#	#	#				
382					#	#	#					#									#	#	#	#	#	#	#	#								
383									#	#	#	#	#									#	#	#									#	#	#	#
384					#	#	#	#					#	#									#	#	#	#								#	#	
385									#	#	#	#	#	#	#	#									#	#	#	#	-							
390	#	#	#	#									#								#	#	#	#	#	#	#	#								
Total no. [#]	7	4	3	2	10	9	8	7	5	7	11	13	11	6	4	3	6	8	8	8	5	8	10	11	13	7	6	6	3	5	5	5	2	6	7	7

For definition of size groups see Table 3 - 13. - [b]The factor price ratio y = wage rate/price of capital. The highest value of y was calculated using the average market wage rate in manufacturing and an assumed interest rate of 10 per cent.

Source: United Nations (UN) (1979), The 1973 World Programme of Industrial Statistics, Summary of Data from Selected Countries. New York; Biro Pusat Statistik (BPS) (Indonesia), 1974/75 Industrial Census. Jakarta, 1976-1978; Department of Statistics (Malaysia) (1973); National Census and Statistics Office (NCSO) (1975), Summary Statistics of Manufacturing Establishments, Manila, unpublished; Department of Statistics (Singapore) (1979); Tambunlertchai, Loohawenchit (1980).

In the highly developed Singaporean economy, economic efficiency is found in both SIs and MIs irrespective of the assumed factor price ratio. SI are efficient in traditional industries such as leather and leather products (323), wood and cork products (331), furniture (332), and other manufacturing (390) as well as in modern industries such as nonelectrical machinery (382) and professional goods (385). MIs operate efficiently in food processing (311-2), clothing (322), footwear (324), plastic products (356) and metal products (381).

Comparing the results among countries, a pattern that was already emerging from the analysis of technical efficiency becomes discernible. There are several industrial subsectors in Singapore, where SIs are efficient, while MIs are efficient in the same subsectors in Malaysia and in the Philippines. This is the case in leather (323), wood products (331) nonelectrical machinery (382) industries in Malaysia, and wood products (331) and furniture (332) industries in the Philippines. This could mean that in the Singaporean economic environment certain problems can be overcome by SIs which in Malaysia and the Philippines can be mastered only by MIs. A similar pattern can be found in industries in which MIs are efficient in Singapore but in which only LIs are efficient in the two other countries - e.g., food processing (311-2), clothing (322), footwear (324), and metal products (381). There are several industries, however, in which SMIs have little chance of becoming efficient for technical reasons, such as electrical machinery, automobiles or other such products, the production of which is strongly affected by increasing returns to scale [13].

The observed differences in relative economic efficiency among countries indicate that SMIs can play an important role in industrial development, even at advanced levels of industrialization such as in Singapore. Industrialization and income growth create new opportunities for SMIs, but create challenges as well. Survival in increasingly competitive domestic markets requires an upgrading of production technologies and product quality as well as adjustment in the output mix. Policies that facilitate implementation of new technologies and new products may effectively support SMI development, while policies simply inducing an increased supply could easily fail. If additional supply of SMIs is not met by expanding demand, as is often the case in narrow markets for traditional goods, falling prices would reduce economic efficiency and jeopardize expansion of the SMI sector. This evaluation follows from the subsequent analysis of supply and demand conditions in markets for final and intermediate products and in export markets.

The findings with respect to efficient SMI resource use demand an important qualification before any policy conclusions can be drawn. The results obtained in the above analysis are still incomplete since they are based solely on actually observed values of prices. No allowance has been made for price distortions, in particular policy-induced price distortions, which may affect establishments of different sizes in different ways and therefore have an impact on the relative economic efficiency of size groups. The analysis of efficiency has been based on census data. Value added is residually derived from data on output and intermediate inputs, and capital data refer to fixed assets, all valued at prices the establishments are actually facing. If preferential trade and investment policies are biased in favor of larger establishments, larger establishments may incur lower input and capital costs than small establishments or enjoy higher output prices. Value added and the factors of production are priced differently among size groups in such a situation. If SMIs enjoy the same preferences as larger establishments, value added in the SMI sector would be higher and capital costs lower. Efficiency of resource use would increase in this sector and the above-stated technical inefficiency of some SMIs could disappear. Also, SMIs could become economically efficient in more industries than stated above; this would be the case when the efficiency of LIs is largely based on preferential treatment.

The size-specific incidence of industrialization policies applied in ASEAN countries is evaluated in Chapters 5 and 6; the subsequent Chapter 4 briefly discusses the growth potential of SMIs. This issue can be regarded as an extension of the analysis of efficiency. If SMIs are to play an important role in industrialization, they have to adjust to changing factor prices and market conditions. Speed and direction of structural adjustment in the SMI sector is influenced by both industrialization and SMI promotion policies. Therefore, the growth potential of SMIs has to be identified to analyze the policy impact.

NOTES

1. A drastic deviation from this pattern concerns cottage and household industries in Thailand. However, the relatively small sample survey, from which factor intensities are derived, does not adequately cover this group of industries. See Footnote 3 in Chapter 2.

52

2. A "technology" is defined as the set of all techniques of production that can be used to produce a certain good and that correspond to the same "level" of scientific and technical development. Thus, one can talk about "traditional", "intermediate", or "modern" technology.

3. See e.g. Griliches (1967, p. 293).

4. See Tambunlertchai, Loohawenchit (1980).

5. This conclusion follows from data on foreign ownership provided in the Industrial Census 1973. See Department of Statistics (Malaysia), Census of Manufacturing Industries, Peninsular Malaysia (1973).

6. It should be recalled that data on establishments with one to four persons engaged are not available for Singapore. Data on capital inputs are not available for establishments with five to nine persons engaged.

7. There are exceptions to these general observations, such as the SIs in the electrical machinery industries of Malaysia and Singapore which are more capital-intensive than LIs. For the sake of the general argument, such exceptions, which are negligible in number, are not further analyzed.

8. Some qualifications will be discussed later in this section.

9. Exceptions are the beverages, textiles, and pottery and earthenware industries in the Philippines and the paper, industrial chemicals, and pottery and earthenware industries in Malaysia.

10. See Warr (1981).

11. For the purpose of the following analysis, no distinction between the size groups LI1 and LI2 is made. In order to economize on space, factor input coefficients for the aggregate size group of LIs are not reproduced in this paper.

12. In the theory of production, the term "technical inefficiency" usually applies to all factor combinations above the unit value isoquant of a linear homogeneous production function. In this paper, the term indicates size groups which use, on an average, more of both factors of production than other size groups.

13. This statement requires the qualification that SMIs may become efficient producers of parts and components for heavy engineering products. To establish this possibility, a much more disaggregated product classification than the one employed in this study would have to be applied.

4
The Growth Potential
of SMIs

The observed differences in relative economic efficiency among countries indicate that SMIs can play an important role in industrial development, even at advanced levels of industrialization such as in Singapore. Industrialization and income growth create new opportunities for SMIs, but create challenges as well. Survival in increasingly competitive domestic markets requires an upgrading of production technologies and product quality as well as adjustment in the output mix. Policies that facilitate implementation of new technologies and new products may effectively support SMI development while policies simply inducing an increased supply could easily fail. If additional supply of SMIs is not met by expanding demand, as is often the case in narrow markets for traditional goods, falling prices would reduce economic efficiency and jeopardize expansion of the SMI sector. This evaluation follows from the subsequent analysis of supply and demand conditions in markets for final and intermediate products and in export markets.

Concerning domestic markets for final products, potential growth of the SMI sector depends on demand expansion and on consumers' preferences. With regard to the latter, it is essential whether consumers regard SMI products as similar to LI products. If products are sufficiently similar, SMIs can capture a larger share of the market by offering lower prices. It is, however, questionable, whether there are many sufficiently homogeneous consumer goods. Anecdotal evidence suggests that usually this is not the case. Chee, for example, found that in Malaysia competition is most intense among establishments of similar size and that many small producers supply customers from low-income groups and rural areas [1]. Under such conditions expansion of demand for consumer goods produced by SMIs depends largely on income growth within relevant groups of consumers and on income elasticities. For some goods, such as building materials, income elasticities tend to be high, but most goods produced for local markets satisfy daily needs and are characterized by

low price and income elasticities. If income is growing
slowly, there is little room in domestic final demand
for growth of the SMI sector, even if special promotion
policies are adopted by governments. Some scope for
expansion exists, however, if SMIs are able to detect
and develop new, specialized markets not served by LIs
because of small market size, special consumers' preferences, remoteness or similar reasons.

It is a general phenomenon in developing countries
that specialization among establishments of different
size is not pronounced [2]; SMIs thus have considerable
growth potential, at least in the long run, provided
SMIs become competitive and reliable. Subcontracting of
simple components and processing activities to SMIs is
potentially advantageous for LIs as subcontracting can
improve flexibility and reduce production costs, while
SMIs can benefit from increasing returns to scale by
supplying the same product to a number of LIs. That
SMIs in most ASEAN countries have not yet developed
this potential, may be due to two basic factors: economic policies may directly or indirectly discriminate
against subcontracting arrangements [3]; and/or SMIs
may find it hard to meet quality standards and
reliability requirements. These problems are not insur-
mountable, as has recently been shown in the case of
Singapore, where in a conducive economic environment
SMIs have managed to become accepted as subcontractors
for the large electronics manufacturers [4].

Concerning the export potential of SMIs, a relevant point is the extent to which SMIs can become
competitive in world markets [5]. A priori considerations suggest that SMIs have considerable export
potential in processing spatially dispersed raw
materials and in producing traditional craft products
as well as other labor- or raw material-intensive products. There is empirical evidence that such a potential
was successfully exploited in many ASEAN countries. In
Singapore, establishments with 10-29 persons engaged
exported 24 per cent of their total sales in 1978,
while establishments with 30-49 persons engaged exported even 43 per cent of their total sales. Singaporean
SIs were most active in exporting food, leather, printing, and nonmetallic mineral products [6]. Moreover,
contrary to widespread belief, exports produced by SMIs
in Malaysia and Thailand are not negligible either. For
Malaysia, the results of a sample survey (399 observations) done in 1973 show that the export share of
total SMI sales was at 12 to 13 per cent, against about
27 per cent for LIs [7]. Malaysia's SMI-produced
exports were concentrated in natural resource-based and
craft industries. The results of a sample survey (1094
observations) done in Thailand in 1976 also show fairly
high SMI export shares: 27 per cent for SIs and 21 per
cent for MIs. Establishments with 100-199 persons

engaged exported 34 per cent of sales, while the figure for larger establishments was only 25 per cent [8].

These data show that SMIs were able to compete with LIs in international markets to a varying degree. The export performance could result from differences in comparative advantage among size groups or from policy induced advantage of one size group against another. An evaluation of these possibilities is part of the policy analysis presented in the next two chapters.

From the preceding discussion it must be concluded that SMIs do not have much scope for growth in their traditional markets, i.e. catering for low-income groups and rural areas. What is required is innovation in products, techniques, and marketing strategy. Differences in the performance of SMIs among ASEAN countries suggest that the economic environment including policies has an important role to play in deciding whether SMIs are victims or agents of economic development. The size-specific influence of industrialization policies in ASEAN countries is investigated in the subsequent Chapter 5. This evaluation is then contrasted with a review of SMI promotion policies (Chapter 6) in order to determine whether there was policy-induced discrimination against SMI development in these countries.

NOTES

1. See Chee (1975, p. 189).
2. See for example Staley, Morse (1965, p. 249).
3. As is the case in the Philippines. See Hill (1981).
4. See Lim, Pang (1981). On the other hand, it is interesting to note that subcontracting has not yet played a major role for SMI development in Korea and Taiwan. See Ho (1980, p. 48).
5. See Bruch (1980).
6. See Bruch (1982c).
7. See Bruch (1980). The sample survey had been conducted by Chee Peng Lim (Universiti Malaya) in 1974.
8. See Sanguanruang et al. (1978, p. 19).

5
The Impact of Economic Policy Measures on the Development of SMIs

Part 1: Foreign Trade Policies and **Investment** Promotion

The importance of macroeconomic **and sector** policies for economic development has **been demonstrated in** numerous country studies as well as **in many comparative** studies [1], but the plantsize-specific impact of economic policies has been neglected. Policy measures do not only affect relative factor and product prices but can also interfere with the functioning of markets. The subsequent analysis will show that some foreign trade and investment promotion policies as well as some monetary and credit policies applied in ASEAN countries were biased against the development of smaller establishments. These policies favored expansion of LIs while limiting SMI markets, impeding technological upgrading of SMIs and depressing profitability in the small-scale sector.

Import tariffs and quantitative restrictions raise the domestic prices of commodities above world market prices. Trade barriers protect domestic producers and discriminate against intermediate and final domestic demand. The net effect on the value added of domestic producers is reflected in the respective rates of effective protection (EPRs). These net effects, however, may differ not only among industries, but also between establishments of different size [2]. Such plantsize-specific effects are aggravated if certain trade policy measures do not apply equally to all establishments within an industrial subsector. Similar effects may result from investment promotion measures depending on the focus of the adopted policy mix.

An analysis of the impact of the various foreign trade and investment promotion policies on the development of SMIs must draw upon a detailed review of such measures in ASEAN countries, which cannot be provided within the scope of this study. However, reviews of industrialization strategies applied in ASEAN countries are available in a number of studies [3]. The following discussion will focus on those features of industrial-

57

ization strategies which are closely related to SMI
development.

(a)   The Structure of Effective Protection

With the exception of Singapore, protection of
domestic producers against foreign competition is still
a dominant feature of industrialization strategies in
ASEAN countries [4]. Nominal rates of protection (NPRs)
for imported capital goods, raw materials and intermediate products usually are relatively low, but are
relatively high for nontraditional consumer goods [5].
In Malaysia in 1974, average nominal protection amounted to 7 per cent for primary industries, 20.8 per cent
for intermediate goods, and 37.4 per cent for consumer
goods, while nominal protection of capital goods
industries was 10.4 per cent [6]. Such a "cascading"
structure of NPRs, which also characterizes import
protection in Indonesia, the Philippines, and Thailand,
results in a structure of effective protection (EPR),
which discriminates against the domestic production of
intermediate and capital goods while favoring producers
of consumer goods. The highest average effective protection is granted to the relatively capital-intensive
production of durable consumer goods.
A comparison of the structure of EPRs and the size
distribution of establishments in ASEAN countries
reveals that effective protection tends to be particularly high in industries where SMI shares in production
are relatively low. Such a negative correlation between
EPRs and production shares was found for Indonesia,
when EPR estimates for 1971 were compared to plant size
structure based on Sensus Industri 1974/75 data [7]. In
the case of Malaysia, von Rabenau has shown that average plant size is much higher in highly protected industries (EPR > 100 per cent) than in less-protected
industries [8]. A similar pattern was found by Anderson
and Khambata for the Philippines, where 80 per cent of
workers in CIs were engaged in industries with low or
negative effective protection (EPR ≤ 25 per cent),
while only 45 per cent of workers were employed in
larger establishments in that category [9].
These findings suggest that the structure of protection tends to favor factor absorption and output
growth in those industries in which large establishments predominate. It should be noted that the importance of large-scale production in industries such as
food processing or consumer durables is in itself partly the result of trade policies accompanied by an artificial lowering of capital cost through credit policies
(see Sections 1 (c) and 2). Import protection and cheap
credit have provided an incentive for both domestic and
foreign investors to establish large capital-intensive

production units sheltered against foreign competition that can crowd out smaller domestic suppliers.

Distortions in resource allocation resulting from differential EPRs among industrial subsectors have other important side-effects on SMI development. Little or no effective protection means a relative discrimination of intermediate and capital goods industries vis-a-vis other industrial subsectors. The policy-induced discrimination impedes output expansion in these activities and increases import demand for intermediate and capital goods. In a free trade situation or in a situation with a uniform nominal tariff rate, domestic producers of these goods would be able to capture a higher share of domestic demand. This also implies that the structure of effective protection prevailing in ASEAN countries is limiting the scope for subcontracting between SMI suppliers and LIs [10].

When effective protection is biased towards capital-intensive, large-scale industries, import protection also discriminates against the use of labor, slowing employment creation and growth of wage income [11]. Although not being entirely the result of trade policies, it is important to note that rapid industrial output expansion in ASEAN countries in the 1970s was not accompanied by rapid creation of industrial employment, except in Singapore. Industrial employment growth did not exceed growth of the labor force by a significant margin though employment creation in manufacturing gained momentum, particularly in Malaysia, in the late 1970s. Industrial output growth in ASEAN countries was primarily achieved by increasing industrial labor productivity, which on average accounted for roughly two-thirds of total industrial growth; this compares with one-third in East Asian developing countries (Hong Kong, Rep. of Korea, Rep. of China) during the same period. Sluggish demand, particularly for unskilled labor, entails slow growth of wage income and, hence, of final demand of low-income groups, which are important customers of SMIs in the consumer goods industries.

The structure of effective protection in ASEAN countries, except for Singapore, is biased against not only certain industries, but also against SMIs within individual industries. In most cases, the present system of protection is not so much a reflection of deliberate policies in accordance with clear objectives, but rather the result of a case-by-case approach to the setting of tariff rates [12]. Due to their relative importance and better access to influential administrators, LIs are likely to be more successful than SMIs in arranging government protection against external competition. Since protection is granted against imports of specific products and since manufacturing industries produce a number of different

products, LIs may be able to arrange import protection
but SMIs in the same industry may not if LIs and SMIs
differ with respect to their product mix. The lack of
sufficiently disaggregated data does not permit EPR
estimates for different size groups of establishments
within individual industries. The hypothesis of differential EPRs among establishments of different size in
individual industries can, however, be supported by a
more detailed analysis of nontariff trade barriers.

(b) The Role of Quantitative Import Restrictions

The structure of NPRs and EPRs is a result of
import tariffs, quantitative restrictions and other
nontariff trade barriers. A system of protection mainly
based on quantitative import restrictions has an in-
built .tendency to discriminate against SMIs more
directly than a system based on the imposition of tariffs. Import controls cause price distortions between
the recipients and the nonrecipients of import
licenses, and under actual conditions, the allocation
of licenses will most likely be biased in favor of LIs;
SMIs will probably find it difficult and costly to
satisfy the bureaucratic requirements for obtaining
licenses. This is the case in particular for SMI appli-
cants located far away from national capitals, a special locational disadvantage. SMI must either forgo
imported inputs or resort to black markets.
It can be expected that foreign exchange and
import controls are most harmful to nontraditional SMIs
which, in general, depend to a substantially larger
degree on imported inputs than do enterprises using
traditional technologies. Difficulties in obtaining
required inputs or capital goods are also likely to
discourage nontraditional SMIs from upgrading production techniques and improving output mixes.
Quantitative import controls have played an important role in trade policies of Indonesia, Malaysia and
the Philippines [13]. In Malaysia, such measures were
introduced only in the late 1960s to supplement tar-
iff-based import substitution policies [14], but such
policies were dominant features of the structure of
incentives in Indonesia and the Philippines in the
first phases of industrialization. In Indonesia, foreign exchange controls and quantitative import restrictions were used extensively till 1965 [15]. During the
subsequent liberalization of economic activities, many
quantitative restrictions were phased out but some
remained in operation, in particular to protect modern
industries such as transport equipment. In the Philippines, a system of rigid foreign exchange controls and
quantitative import restrictions was introduced in 1949
for balance-of-payments reasons and soon became an

integral part of an industrialization strategy aimed at providing effective protection especially to consumer goods industries [16].

The above considerations suggest that primarily nontraditional SMIs were put at a significant disadvantage by these policies in both Indonesia and the Philippines right from the beginning of the industrialization process [17]. Although discrimination of SMIs through quantitative controls was less important in the late 1960s and early 1970s - when the protective system was mainly based on tariffs - the effect of quantitative controls may still be reflected in the relatively low shares of SIs and, particularly, MIs in manufacturing value added, which is shown in Table 2-3 for Indonesia and the Philippines in the 1970s.

(c)   Investment and Export Promotion

By the late 1960s it was widely felt in ASEAN countries that the phase of "easy" import substitution was approaching its end and that industrial policies had to be reoriented. However, instead of removing trade barriers, the existing structure of incentives was supplemented by additional measures intended to actively promote industrial investment and exports [18]. Common elements of these incentive packages were:

-   the reduction of or exemptions from duties on imported inputs,
-   import duty drawbacks for exporters,
-   tax incentives,
-   concessional export credit facilities.

SMIs are hardly among the beneficiaries of these incentives, which are selectively granted on application, either because they are explicitly excluded or because they find bureaucratic requirements and procedures too tedious to satisfy. The working of these regulations and their quantitative significance varies among ASEAN countries.

In Indonesia, the Foreign Investment Law of 1967 and the Domestic Investment Law of 1968 provide for duty exemptions on imported capital goods and intermediate goods and grant exemptions from corporate income tax for the first five years after production has begun. For the second five years of operation, a 50 per cent reduction on duties and taxes is granted. Additional benefits are accelerated depreciation allowances and partial deduction of investment costs from taxable income. These incentives artificially lower the price of capital vis-a-vis labor and promote relatively capital-intensive lines of production, in which large establishments predominate.

Analysis of guidelines applied in Malaysia indicates that SMIs can be effectively excluded from preferences such as exemptions from duties on capital goods imports [19]. Only establishments with licenses under the Industrial Coordination Act can apply for exemptions, though such a license is not required for establishments with fewer than 25 fulltime employees or less than M$ 250,000 in assets. The applicant must import the capital good directly, but SMIs usually purchase their capital goods from trading companies. The respective capital good must not be available from a domestic supplier, but SMIs often use simple or intermediate technology, which is also produced locally. Finally, capital goods must be brand-new, but for SMIs, in many cases used machinery is more adequate.

The first requirement also applies to duty-free imports of raw materials and intermediate goods. According to recent estimates, such exemptions from import duties are extremely important in Malaysia. According to Malaysian Industrial Development Authority (MIDA) in 1975 about 50 per cent of import duties were not collected because of such exemptions. In 1978 about one-fourth of all capital goods were exempted from import duties [20].

While exemptions from import duties are intended to provide a higher degree of effective protection to import-competing industries as well as to make export industries more competitive on world markets, import duty drawbacks serve the sole purpose of reducing discrimination against export establishments. These drawbacks, however, are granted only when finished products are exported directly. This implies that indirect exporters - the actual or potential suppliers of components - are excluded and the development of backward linkages from exporters of finished products to mostly small- and medium-sized subcontractors is discouraged. Similar effects can be attributed to export credits that commercial banks can refinance at concessional rates at the Malaysian Central Bank (Bank Negara) because preshipment credit is available to direct exporters only. Post-shipment credit is limited to exports exceeding M$ 30,000 in value [21]. Because of this limit, SMIs may be excluded from the credit scheme even if they are exporting directly.

Tax incentives provided under the Investment Incentives Act of 1968 and its amendments largely favor capital-intensive LIs, as shown in Table 5-1. This table provides information on projects in manufacturing industries approved by MIDA. In most years since 1970, projects without incentives (WI) were much smaller in terms of planned employment than investment projects which qualified for incentives. Similarly, with the exception of 1979 and 1980, projects without incentives were on average less capital-intensive than projects

Table 5-1: Malaysia[a] – Structure of Selected Investment Incentives[b], 1970–1981

Incentive[c]	1970	1971	1972	1973	1974	1975	1976	1977	1978	1979	1980	1981
No. of approved projects												
Total	334	305	355	473	525	461	425	400	428	484	412	519
Share of potential employment (per cent)												
LI	-	-	-	-	-	13.6	2.9	10.2	11.6	7.0	1.1	4.4
LUR	-	-	-	-	4.6	3.3	3.1	5.5	2.9	1.2	1.2	1.4
PS	72.0	60.9	72.2	60.4	52.6	25.4	46.4	36.7	36.2	50.0	53.9	33.1
ITC	8.6	18.9	4.7	10.3	13.4	11.4	14.6	9.7	17.8	7.0	12.3	16.3
WI	18.7	14.7	17.8	20.0	28.4	42.6	31.5	37.6	31.5	34.8	31.5	44.1
Total (actual)	47,232	48,717	56,449	81,510	71,378	36,171	32,265	29,632	36,892	53,474	41,558	52,356
Average number of employees/project												
LI	-	-	-	-	-	491.9	135.0	216.5	328.2	311.6	119.3	232.0
LUR	-	-	255.9	264.1	219.2	92.5	142.6	148.4	175.8	166.5	246.0	355.0
PS	196.5	197.9	257.9	275.0	226.2	96.7	142.7	111.0	121.3	252.2	266.7	196.6
ITC	131.3	418.0	264.7	323.6	308.3	98.0	62.0	51.5	91.1	61.0	75.2	109.6
WI	69.5	62.5	54.5	69.0	66.5	53.5	45.5	53.5	51.6	61.8	51.5	68.1
Total (average)	141.4	159.7	159.0	172.3	136.0	78.5	75.9	74.1	86.2	110.5	100.9	100.9
Average capital[d] intensity (1,000 M$/employee)												
LI	-	-	-	-	-	75.4	54.4	64.6	11.1	18.5	10.8	15.7
LUR	-	-	7.2	6.6	6.5	17.9	7.9	29.0	1.8	9.5	5.1	4.6
PS	24.3	27.0	13.9	17.6	30.2	30.9	33.2	19.5	27.0	11.4	11.3	23.5
ITC	24.6	19.3	23.4	16.6	20.1	67.3	44.0	31.5	37.6	36.1	24.2	48.6
WI	23.5	20.6	12.2	14.2	25.8	24.6	23.4	13.4	15.3	61.2	21.0	21.0
Total (average)	24.1	26.8	14.1	15.8	26.3	37.8	31.7	23.8	22.6	30.9	15.9	26.2

[a] Including Sabah and Sarawak. – [b] Other incentives not specified are included in total. – [c] LI: Locational incentives, LUR: Labor Utilization Relief, PS: Pioneer Status, ITC: Investment Tax Credit, WI: Without incentive. – [d] Approved capital.

Source: Malaysian Industrial Development Authority (MIDA), Annual Report. Kuala Lumpur, various issues.

receiving incentives [22]. The single most important
tax incentive in Malaysia is the so-called "Pioneer
Status" (PS), under which an establishment is exempted
from corporate income tax for a specified number of
years. The tax exempted period increases with the
amount of capital invested. It is not surprising that
the share of pioneer establishments in total establishments of the same size group is increasing with plant
size (Table 5-2). Except for establishments with 500
and more persons engaged, pioneer establishments are
also found to be more capital-intensive than other
establishments of similar size.

In the Philippines, despite weak growth performance of manufacturing industries and persistent balance-of-payments problems in the late 1960s, a major
policy shift toward an outward-looking strategy did not
occur in the Philippines until 1980. The Industrial
Incentives Act of 1967 supplemented by the Export
Incentives Act of 1970 provide some duty exemptions on
imported inputs and various tax incentives [23]. In
contrast to Malaysia, where such incentives have been
applied extensively, incentives have remained relatively unimportant in the Philippines in terms of the
number of beneficiaries (Table 5-3) as well as with
respect to their impact on effective protection of
manufacturing industries.

In examining their effect on EPRs, Tan [24] found
that such incentives caused only negligible changes.
For a small number of beneficiaries, however, duty
exemptions and tax preferences may still mean a significant subsidy that could offset the discriminating
effect of the protective system against exports. Among
the beneficiaries of the preferences, however, there
were relatively few small- and medium-sized enterprises, as is revealed in Table 5-3. Assuming a book
value of fixed assets in SMIs of up to ₱ 2.5 million
[25], less than one-quarter of the promoted projects
were related to SMIs until the end of 1977.

In Singapore, investment and export promotion
policies were at least as important as in Malaysia. A
difference is that Singapore basically is a free-trade
area; investment incentives have been mostly of fiscal
nature, e.g., exemptions from corporate income tax.
Since May 1975, subsidized export credit has also been
made available [26]. Although information on the recipients of tax incentives is confidential, it seems safe
to say that only fairly large export-oriented firms
were the main beneficiaries [27].

In Thailand, SMIs have also been effectively
excluded from investment and export promotion, as
provided in the Investment Promotion Act and the Export
Promotion Act of 1972, which include incentives similar
to those of other ASEAN countries: duty exemptions, tax

Table 5-2: Malaysia - Relative Importance of Pioneer Establishments by Size, 1973

Size (persons engaged)	Shares of pioneer establishments (per cent)					Indices[b]	
	No. of establishments	No. of persons engaged[a]	Fixed assets	Value added	Capital intensity	Capital productivity	Labor productivity
1 - 9	0.1	0.2	3.7	1.8	18.5	0.5	8.4
10 - 19	1.3	1.4	6.6	2.5	4.7	0.4	1.8
20 - 29	3.2	3.3	15.6	8.2	4.7	0.5	2.5
30 - 49	4.6	5.1	16.3	11.5	3.2	0.7	2.3
50 - 99	12.1	12.9	34.0	17.4	2.6	0.5	1.4
100 - 199	25.7	26.1	40.8	36.5	1.6	0.9	1.4
200 - 499	45.5	48.4	60.0	52.5	1.2	0.9	1.1
500 - 999	57.1	57.4	58.2	52.0	1.0	0.9	0.9
1000 +	61.9	67.0	63.1	57.4	0.9	0.9	0.9
Total	3.2	7.4	46.9	37.1	6.3	0.8	5.0

[a] Part-time workers were given a weight of 0.5. - [b] Value for pioneer establishments/value for all establishments in the respective size group.

Source: Department of Statistics (Malaysia) (1973).

Table 5-3: Philippines - Plant Size Distribution of Promoted
Projects Registered by the Bureau of Investment
in December 1977 (No. of Projects)

Plant size (assets in ₱ million)	Total	Processing of agricult. raw materials	Processing of mineral raw materials	Metal Products	Chemi- cals	Others
1	22	4	1	11	6	-
1- 4	88	39	10	32	4	3
4-10	100	55	11	20	12	2
10-50	159	93	23	24	13	6
50+	64	22	20	3	19	-
Total	433	213	65	90	54	11

Source: Information received from the Board of Investments
(Philippines).

incentives, and protection against foreign competition
[28]. Exclusion of SMIs from these provisions results
not only from tedious administrative procedures, but
also from a policy explicitly promoting LIs [29]. This
policy is reflected in the fact that in 1975 each promoted establishment employed on average more than 400
workers [30].

(d) Conclusions

The following general conclusions can be drawn
from the preceding discussion: first, the structure of
effective protection in ASEAN countries (except Singapore) seems to have benefitted LIs more than SMIs. LIs
are concentrated in industries with relatively high
ERPs, while SMIs and CIs are concentrated in industries
with relatively low or even negative ERPs. Second,
selective measures with regard to individual enterprises tend to aggravate the policy-induced discrimination of SMIs vis-a-vis LIs. Such measures comprise
foreign exchange and import controls, selective tariff
protection on a case-by-case basis, exemptions from
import duties, tax incentives, and subsidized export
credit. Third, the protective system as well as additional selective measures have negative repercussions
on the growth potential of SMIs. These impede an
upgrading of technology and improvement in product
quality and output mix. Domestic demand for SMI
products is negatively affected in two ways: import
protection creates a bias against the use of labor,
which retards growth of demand for consumer goods; and
preferences granted for the use of imported inter-

mediate and capital goods divert intermediate demand of
LIs from local to import markets. With respect to
industrial exports, SMIs suffer from an artificial
disadvantage because incentives, which could compensate
for the discrimination of exports through import
protection, are focused on the needs of LIs.

It can further be concluded that market prices
used in Chapter 3 to evaluate the relative efficiency
of small, medium, and large establishments are distort-
ed. In general, the price of value added will be higher
in LIs than in SMIs, while the price of capital goods
will be lower. Thus, from the point of view of social
cost-benefit analysis, SIs and MIs are likely to be
more efficient than indicated in Chapter 3. Quantitative estimates of policy-induced price distortions
would, however, require further detailed country analysis.

Part 2: Monetary and Credit Policies

Even in industrialized countries, problems of
financing capital needs are generally more difficult
for SMIs to overcome than for LIs. This is all the more
true in the case in developing countries where financial markets are fragmented and underdeveloped. When
commercial credit is extremely scarce or not available,
smaller and, especially, traditional establishments
must resort to internal funds or to informal financial
markets (family, friends, money-lenders, suppliers,
etc.). It can be argued that in financing traditional
activities, informal credit markets have advantages
over formal markets, such as a higher degree of flexibility and lower transaction costs because of a more
intimate knowledge of local conditions. It must be
stressed, however, that informal markets are overtaxed
by financing nontraditional SMI activities, since
informal loans are usually limited to very small
amounts and to short pay-off periods. Furthermore,
informal markets tend to be of a local nature and their
capability for mobilization of savings, refinancing,
and term transformation is limited. Hence, access to
commercial credit is essential for the development and
upgrading of the SMI sector.

The level of development of financial markets in
ASEAN countries is illustrated in Table 5-4 by the
ratio of time and savings desposits to GNP; this ratio
is usually regarded as a rough indicator for financial
deepening [31]. Table 5-4 shows that financial deepening is most advanced in Singapore, and that in Malaysia
financial markets have improved rapidly and that the
country was able to reach a level of financial development similar to Singapore in the late 1970s. Financial
markets are much less developed in the other ASEAN

Table 5-4: ASEAN Countries: Ratio of Time and Savings Deposits[a] and GNP (per cent)

Year	Indonesia	Malaysia	Philippines	Singapore	Thailand
1966	–	14.1	12.8	–	14.1
1967	–	15.8	14.2	–	15.9
1968	0.6	17.9	13.8	42.7	17.4
1969	1.9	21.0	14.1	44.4	18.7
1970	2.5	23.4	13.5	45.7	20.5
1971	4.1	26.6	13.0	45.2	23.2
1972	5.2	28.7	12.0	45.7	26.3
1973	5.1	28.6	11.7	44.8	24.8
1974	5.2	43.4[b]	10.0	44.2	24.6
1975	6.1	52.0	12.0	47.5	26.8
1976	6.9	54.0	13.9	51.5	28.9
1977	6.2	54.3	15.5	52.6	30.9
1978	6.2	58.7	17.6	54.2	30.1
1979	6.0	59.4	16.5	52.7	30.2
1980	6.2	64.3	17.1	64.8	30.7
1981	6.2	72.6	18.7	70.6	32.5

[a] Time and savings deposits of the private sector in commercial banks and other financial institutions. - [b] Prior to 1974 Employees Provident Fund not included.

Source: International Monetary Fund (1980, June 1983).

countries. There was an increase of time and savings deposits in Thailand in the 1966/79 period, but financial deepening stagnated in the Philippines and even more so in Indonesia [32]. While SMIs potentially have easier access to comercial credit in countries with highly developed financial markets such as Malaysia and Singapore than in countries where commercial credit is generally very scarce, the actual access of SMIs to commercial credit is largely determined by monetary and credit policies. To understand this relationship, the determinants of credit supply have to be discussed briefly.

Transaction costs are a crucial variable in establishing commercial credit availability for SMIs. Transaction costs consist of administrative costs plus allowance for the default risk. The two cost elements are characterized by a trade-off relationship, i.e. the default risk can be reduced by more thorough evaluation of applications for credit thus entailing higher administrative costs. The transaction cost is equal to the mark-up on the cost for funds required by financial institutions to break even in lending operations. For several reasons, lending to SMIs tends to involve higher transaction costs than for lending to LIs [33]. First, accounting is inadequate in many SMIs and audited statements are only rarely available making evaluation of the standing of a potential borrower difficult for traditional lending institutions. Secondly, the default risk in lending to SMIs may actually be higher than in lending to LIs, especially when the prospective borrower is not well-established. Thirdly, the risk of lending to SMIs may be overestimated by financial institutions with little experience with this type of borrower. In such a case, lending institutions will attach high priority to collateral and relatively low weight to the viability of the project to be financed; many SMIs however, lack collateral. And finally, there are other problems such as low quality of management, overestimation of demand, vulnerability of operations to sickness or death of the entrepreneur, or dependence on only a few customers.

Transaction costs, however, do not depend only on borrower characteristics, but also on the experience of financial institutions in lending to SMIs. The extent to which financial institutions gain such experience is related to the structure of financial markets. This structure is heavily influenced, if not determined, by government intervention. A high degree of competition may force institutions to look more actively among SMIs for new customers and to regard initially high transaction costs, which cannot be entirely recovered by interest payments, as an investment in future experience. Such entrepreneurial behavior is excluded when financial markets are highly regulated and when financial institutions are run like bureaucracies.

Another aspect concerns the freedom of financial institutions to charge differential interest rates according to differences in transaction costs among borrowers. A system of administered interest rates with relatively low interest rate ceilings may help borrowers with good standing obtain investible funds at low cost, but may effectively exclude other qualified borrowers from commercial credit. Interest rate ceilings may, therefore, prevent financial institutions from accumulating experience and from adapting their procedures to the needs of a vast number of small potential borrowers.

Whether low interest-rate ceilings effectively impede SMIs' access to institutional credit is subject of a controversy. An assessment of credit markets and financial policies in ASEAN countries does, however, provide rather clear indications of the relationship between market regulation and credit availability for SMIs.

Salient features of the Indonesian financial sector are the overwhelming role of the Central Bank (Bank Indonesia) and the predominance of the state in commercial banking. Bank Indonesia is administering a complex system of interest rates on deposits and loans of five state commercial banks [34]. They are virtually the only domestic source of medium- and long-term credit as Bank Indonesia subsidizes their interest rates on time and savings deposits and provides refinancing facilities at concessional terms. Since April 1974 credit of commercial banks is subject to a comprehensive system of specific ceilings. This system has significantly reduced competition among state banks. Direct controls became necessary because rediscounting facilities had been exhausted by a policy of channelling concessional credit into priority areas [35]. These facilities also serve the purpose of subsidizing the state banks which are suffering from high administrative costs, arrears and credit defaults [36]. As a result of the institutional and regulatory set-up, access to formal credit is rather limited for all those small establishments which are not eligible to special credit programs (to be discussed in the next chapter). Therefore, informal credit markets are a very important source of funds for SMIs in Indonesia.

Similar to the Indonesian situation, the Central Bank of the Philippines is very active in regulating financial activities and in assigning certain functions to certain types of institutions in the Philippines. A recent World Bank study shows that such intervention has contributed to market fragmentation, a low degree of competition among financial institutions, and a lack of medium- and long-term funds [37]. As in the case of Indonesia, rediscounting windows have been assigned the responsibility for allocating credit to priority areas. Interest rates on loans are subject to relatively low ceilings, but interest rates for term and savings deposits have been allowed to rise in order to attract long-term funds in times of high inflation. The narrowing spread has further reduced the ability of financial institutions to provide loans when transaction costs are high, causing interest rates to be largely replaced by transaction costs as determinants of credit allocation. The narrowing spread effectively excluded many small labor-intensive establishments from commercial credit markets. This situation has only slightly improved, when the interest rate on long-term loans was allowed to rise in 1976 from 12-14 per cent to 19 per cent [38]. It remains to be seen whether the complete liberalization of interest rates on medium- and long-term loans, which was effected in July 1981, will result in better access of SMIs to commercial credit.

Quantitative controls and ceilings on interest rates are also pervasive in Thailand. Nominal interest rates have been kept at fairly constant levels, while real interest rates were allowed to fluctuate widely in response to changing rates of inflation. The consequence of this policy was credit rationing according to differences in transaction costs.

In the 1970s, controls and regulations in the financial sector were largely dismantled in Malaysia. The only major exception concerns a few measures designed to improve credit availability for the indigenous population (Bumiputra). The declared objective of deregulation was stimulation of competition among financial institutions and upgrading of their performance and international competitiveness. Prior to 1978, maximum interest rates on deposits and minimum interest rates on loans provided some infant industry protection to the banking sector; however, these rates had been adjusted quite frequently in response to changing market conditions. Since 1978, the only regulated interest rate applied to loans to the Bumiputra and small-scale establishments and for home mortgages. The volume of credit reserved for these purposes is determined by the Central Bank (Bank Negara), and individual financial institutions must comply with the set quotas. It can be concluded that in Malaysia, SMIs do not face the institutional impediments with respect to access to commercial credit observed in other countries. Credit availability results partly from regulations implemented and overseen by the Central Bank and partly from the relatively high level of development of the Malaysian financial sector (Table 5-4) and from competition among financial institutions.

A similar conclusion can be drawn with regard to the case of Singapore. In this country, the financial sector was almost completely liberalized in the 1970s, and interest rate regulations were abolished in 1975. Besides some credit programs of little overall significance, there is no selective credit policy and financial institutions freely compete for customers. Therefore, SMIs' access to commercial credit did not constitute a problem in Singapore. This may also be a reason why the Monetary Authority of Singapore (MAS) does not publish data on loan disbursements by size classes of borrowing establishments which would allow comparisons with other countries. The healthy impact of the financial environment on SMI development is, however, demonstrated by two earlier findings. SMIs in Singapore were more efficient users of resources than SMIs in the other countries (Chapter 3-3), and they grew even faster than LIs in 1973-1978 (Chapter 2-3), when almost all interventions in financial markets had been abolished.

A comparison of ASEAN countries suggests that liberalization of financial markets can improve SMIs' access to commercial credit. Yet, financial liberalization is rather a necessary than a sufficient condition. The availability of credit to SMIs is the combined result of an interest rate mechanism governing the allocation of credit, better performance of financial institutions, and highly competitive financial markets. Although efficiently functioning financial markets are the objective of financial development in the long run, ideal conditions cannot be readily transformed into policy conclusions applicable to specific countries. Even under appropriate financial policies, it is difficult to bridge the gap between the requirements established by formal institutions and the informal nature of many small establishments. As has already been mentioned, high transaction costs in lending to SMIs result not only from a lack of experience of lending institutions, but also from establishment characteristics in the SMI sector. Although elimination of discrimination against SMIs through selective trade and investment policies will be instrumental in upgrading SMI performance and in reducing transaction costs in the long run, interest rates adequately reflecting cost and risk considerations may be extremely high in the short or medium run. Aside from political resistance to large differences in lending rates for small and large enterprises, there is the additional aspect of low-risk borrowers paying for high-risk borrowers if the institutions have not yet developed screening procedures enabling them to distinguish among various risk categories. This is the case because interest and principal of loans in default must be recovered from nondelinquent borrowers.

Because of this externality, Anderson argues that interest rates on SMI loans should reflect the estimated costs of lending to low-risk SMIs [39]. Following this suggestion, financial institutions would have to be subsidized while developing appropriate screening procedures to enable them to apply different interest rates according to risk. It should be noted, however, that on economic grounds, such subsidies are justified only as a supportive measure in a phase of financial liberalization, and their impact on the development of SMIs depends largely on the simultaneous reduction of discrimination against SMIs resulting from other policy measures.

NOTES

1. For an up-to-date overview, see Developing Asia: The Importance of Domestic Policies (Asian Development Bank, 1982).

2. See DiTullio (1974, pp. 80 f.).

3. For an overview see Hiemenz (1982) and the literature cited there.

4. In Singapore such policies were confined to a rather brief and unimportant interlude in the 1960s.

5. For details see the following country studies: Indonesia: Pitt (1981); Malaysia: Hoffmann, Tan (1980); von Rabenau (1976); Philippines: Bautista, Power, Assoc. (1979); Thailand: Akrasanee (1978).

6. See von Rabenau (1976, p. 27).

7. EPR estimates for 1971 were taken from Pitt (1981).

8. See von Rabenau (1976, p. 41 f.).

9. See Anderson, Khambata (1981, p. 120 ff.).

10. The damaging effect of the tariff structure on the development of subcontracting relationships has been analyzed by Hill (1981, p. 17) for the Philippines.

11. The relationship between trade policies and domestic resource use is analyzed in detail in Hiemenz (1982, pp. 29-54) or in Krueger (1978).

12. See e.g. Rhee (1980) on Malaysia.

13. Quantitative controls were important in Thailand until 1955 but were abolished in favor of tariff protection. See Akrasanee (1977). The revised "Investment Promotion Act" of 1977 has, however, authorized the Board of Investment to reimpose import controls in special cases.

14. See Hoffmann, Tan (1980, pp. 52 ff.).

15. See Donges, Stecher, Wolter (1974); McCawley (1979).

16. See Power, Sicat (1971); Baldwin (1975).

17. See Bautista, Power, Assoc. (1979, pp. 62 f.) on the Philippines.

18. A partial exception is Malaysia, where certain industrial estates have been declared free trade areas.

19. See Rhee (1980) on these guidelines.

20. See Rhee (1980).

21. See Rhee (1980). The post-shipment credit facility was introduced in January 1977 and the pre-shipment facility in March 1979.

22. For a detailed description of individual incentives see Spinanger (1980).

23. For details see Gregorio (1979), N.A. Tan (1979).

24. N.A. Tan (1979).

25. This estimate is derived from the average capital intensity of establishments with 50-99 persons engaged multiplied by 100 employees.

26. For details see Singapore International Chamber of Commerce (1979).

27. Informal information from EDB (Economic Development Board).

28. See Visanuvimol (1980, p. 59); Akrasanee (1977, p. 37).

29. See Board of Investment (Thailand, 1979).

30. See Akrasanee (1977, Appendix Table 2.4).

31. See Shaw (1973).

32. The increase in the late 1960s and early 1970s in Indonesia is due to the recovery from the period of hyper-inflation and near-collapse of the economy during the Sukarno era, which ended in 1965.

33. See e.g., Anderson-Saito, Villanueva (1981) on an estimate for the Philippines.

34. Their share in total outstanding loans of the banking system amounted to almost 90 per cent in 1979.

35. See Arndt (1979). In essence, priority areas are agriculture and indigenous (pribumi) establishments as well as public enterprises.

36. See Arndt (1979), Hill (1979).

37. See World Bank (1980, pp. 1 ff.).

38. See Anderson, Khambata (1981).

39. See Anderson (1982, pp. 49 ff.).

6
SMI Promotion Policies

1. Financial Assistance to SMIs

During the 1970s or even earlier, all ASEAN countries have launched programs for financial assistance
to SMIs. This section provides a summary appraisal of
these programs and addresses the following key questions:

(1) The extent to which financial assistance has improved the access of SMIs to institutional credit, i.e., whether these programs can offset the
negative impact of other credit policies.
(2) The extent to which these programs contribute to
the objective of financial market development.
(3) The extent to which SMIs are provided with credit
at concessional terms and what the economic
implications of concessional schemes are.

Design and quantitative relevance of such programs
vary considerably among ASEAN countries; in subsequent
subsections, major elements of financial assistance to
SMIs in each country are presented separately. Some
tentative policy conclusions are then drawn from the
country experiences. These conclusions serve as a
framework for detailed recommendations on SMI promotion
policies.

(a) Indonesia

At present in Indonesia, there are several credit
programs for small- and medium-scale businesses involving short-, medium- and long-term loans for both working capital and investment finance ranging from US-$ 5
to US-$ 120,000.00 [1]. In terms of volume the program
of Small Investment Credit (KIK) and Small Permanent
Working Capital Credit (KMKP) is by far the largest,
with credit outstanding passing the US-$ 1 billion mark
in early 1981. However, only about 12 per cent of these
loans have accrued to manufacturing industries. The
KIK/KMKP program was launched in December 1973 in

response to rising criticism that small establishments had only very limited access to subsidized credit. At present, an industrial establishment is eligible for KIK/KMKP credits if its net worth of assets does not exceed Rp. 100 million (US-$ 160,000) [2] and if it is owned by indigenous people (pribumi) [3]. Maximum loan size under both KIK and KMPK is Rp. 10 million (US-$ 16,000), extendable to Rp. 15 million under certain conditions, but the average size of loans extended to industrial enterprises was much smaller. Loans approved in 1980 amounted to Rp. 4.8 million (US-$ 7,700) on an average in the case of KIK loans and Rp. 3.0 million (US-$ 4,800) in the case of KMKP loans. The maximum maturity period for KIK loans is ten years and three years for KMKP loans, extendable for an additional three years. Interest rates are respectively fixed at 10.5 and 10 per cent. Applications can be filed with the more than 1,000 branch offices of state, provincial and selected private banks handling the program. These banks receive special liquidity credits from Bank Indonesia to finance concessional credit and to participate in credit insurance arrangements, which cover 75 per cent of the default risk. Overall, these arrangements provide a gross interest spread of 6.18 per cent for KIK and roughly 7.13 per cent for KMKP [4].

Table 6-1 shows how lending to SMIs under the KIK/KMKP scheme has expanded over time. After an encouraging start in 1974, lending increased only slowly in subsequent years. Average annual growth rates amounted to about 15-16 per cent in real terms for both KIK and KMKP in the period 1976-1978; thereafter, lending gained momentum and increased at a real average annual growth rate of 44 per cent for KIK and 31 per cent for KMKP in the period 1978-1980 [5]. By the end of the first quarter of 1981, more than 12,500 applications for investment finance and 31,300 applications for working capital credit had been approved.

Despite these impressive absolute figures, the scheme must still expand, if the availability of credit to SMIs is to improve significantly. In 1978, total KIK/KMKP lending accounted for less than 3 per cent of total lending to manufacturing industries, and even after the rapid increase in lending since 1978, this share is not likely to have surpassed the 5 per cent mark. There is no doubt that the KIK/KMKP scheme has improved access of SMIs to institutional finance, but considering that this program is the single most important source of formal credit for SMIs, it must be concluded that SMIs are still at a relative disadvantage with respect to access to funds for investment and working capital purposes.

A comparison of the number of approvals (12,500 and 31,300 respectively) and the number of potential recipients tentatively supports such a conclusion. Ac-

Table 6-1: Indonesia – Annual and Cumulative KIK/KMKP Loan Approvals in Manufacturing, 1974-1981 (1st Quarter)

Year	K I K Annual			K M K.P Annual		
	Cumulative no.	Amount (Rp.mill.)	Share in total (per cent)	Cumulative no.	Amount (Rp. mill.)	Share in total (per cent)
1974	1,739	6,610	23.2	4,546	9,531	33.7
1975	2,930			6,615		
1976	4,341	2,894	14.2	10,135	5,537	22.8
1977	5,444	3,476	14.0	12,895	6,132	19.9
1978	6,486	4,661	14.2	15,138	8,953	17.5
1979	7,859	7,336	12.0	18,676	14,589	13.4
1980	10,879	14,630	10.9	26,693	24,229	11.9
1981						
1st qt.	12,537	3,617	11.2	31,390	5,862	11.0
Total	-	43,224	12.9	-	74,833	15.0

Source: Bank Indonesia (1981), Arief (1981).

cording to the 1974/75 Industrial Census, there are about 155,000 manufacturing establishments with fewer than 50 persons engaged but with at least one paid worker. The target group of the KIK/KMKP scheme, however, is even larger, since an upgrading of the 1.3 million cottage industry units is intended as well. The number of approvals in Table 6-1, on the other hand, must be adjusted downward in order to arrive at the number of recipients because of multiple loans to individual enterprises. Hence, at most 0.1 to 0.2 per cent of all eligible establishments was able to benefit from concessional credit provided by KIK/KMKP.

The performance of the KIK/KMKP scheme over the years reflects a number of problems inherent in concessional financial assistance to SMIs. One reason for the sluggish progress of the scheme until 1978 has been lack of interest on the side of the handling banks due to high arrears [6], problems with the credit insurance agency, lack of adequately trained manpower, lack of familiarity with term loans, and an aversion to unsophisticated clients [7]. The high risk perceived by the banks led to collateral requirements inconsistent with the intentions of the scheme; this is illustrated by the fact that until the end of 1979 only 13 per cent of cumulative KIK loans and 1 per cent of cumulative KMKP loans went to new industrial enterprises [8]. On the other hand, SMI demand for funds was also sluggish in the initial years. Bottlenecks such as lack of technical and market knowledge, lack of entrepreneurial energy, and a reluctance to approach a formal institution may have caused the slow start in SMI credit applications. The scheme has, however, gained momentum in more recent years, when it was supported by the Small Enterprise Development Project (SEDP) launched in 1977 [9]. This project, involving almost US-$ 40 million in technical assistance, focuses on upgrading lending procedures of the handling banks and on training of loan officers.

From an economic point of view the quantitative growth of a credit scheme is not necessarily tantamount to its macroeconomic efficiency. The crucial element of the KIK/KMKP program is not the fact that lending to small establishments is actively promoted, but rather that credit is provided at concessional conditions. There are arguments both in favor and against concessionality in SMI lending. The controversy refers to the relationship between own funds, external finance, and lending conditions. Economic theory suggests that under normal behavioral assumptions, the share of own funds in financing a given project rises with the costs of external funds. This implies that the availability of credit at concessional conditions is likely to reduce the share of self-financing and may divert such funds to nonproductive uses. When access to credit is limited to small amounts at excessively high interest rates in formal markets, the investment project may not be viable at all and diversion of own funds from productive uses would be larger. The proponents of concessional interest rates argue [10] that investment of SMIs is stimulated in the aggregate by low capital costs, that attractive lending conditions are instrumental in overcoming the reluctance of many SMIs to deal with formal institutions at all, and that concessional credit can compensate SMIs for discrimination caused by other industrialization policies.

The validity of any of these suggestions cannot be rejected on a priori grounds. Critics of concessional lending point out that low-interest ceilings destroy the allocation function of interest rates and may lead to suboptimal investment decisions, and that the growth and employment effect of a given amount of investible funds could be lower rather than higher when funds are provided at concessional terms. It is argued that this danger is aggravated if low-cost investment funds lure entrepreneurs into applying advanced technology when the supply of complementary resources is not adequate. Concerning feasibility, it is argued that budgetary costs would be tremendous if concessional credit is to be available to all SMIs over a substantial period of time, and that any concessional scheme is prone to corruption. Also, the concept of concessionality may be considered self-defeating to the extent that inappropriate credit allocation increases arrears. Given a fixed interest spread, banks will either become reluctant to participate in such credit schemes or allocate loans primarily to projects that would be viable at market rates of interest. The effect would be to reduce rather than improve access of SMIs to institutional credit.

These arguments cannot be evaluated individually for the Indonesian case. A few observations, however, seem to be justified in light of the available evidence. The KIK/KMKP program has improved access of CIs and SMIs to institutional credit and, more importantly, has created positive externalities by bridging the gap between formal institutions and customers that had no previous experience with commercial banks. Nonetheless, the program has reached only a small portion of its target group, and it is doubtful that the concessional terms provided under the program have contributed to SMIs' improved access to formal credit. Disbursement was slow during the first four years of the KIK/KMKP program, indicating reluctance by both banks and borrowers towards the program despite the highly concessional interest rates, which were even lower than concessional interest rates granted to large-scale producers [11]. Lending increased substantially only when supported by technical assistance under SEDP (since 1977).

The Indonesian experience suggests that an upgrading of the banks' lending procedures and training of loan officers may be a more effective measure for improving SMIs access to formal credit than concessional terms. Technical assistance projects, which assist in the implementation of SMI credit programs, have the advantage of avoiding the possible negative effects attributed to concessional terms above. This does not mean, however, that subsidized interest rates for SMI lending must be ruled out completely. As was discussed in Chapter 5-2, banks tend to anticipate high transaction costs for SMI lending. Following Anderson's suggestion [12], an interest rate subsidy may be economically justified that reduces interest rates for SMI borrowers to those rates charged to low-risk SMI customers. Such a measure would preserve the banks' flexibility in adjusting lending conditions to project risks and would be consistent with a gradual process of financial liberalization.

(b) The Philippines

Commercial credit is available for only a small minority of small enterprises in the Philippines; most medium- and long-term loans to SMIs are provided by the public Development Bank of the Philippines (DBP) and by the Central Bank under the Industrial Guarantee and Loan Fund (IGLF) program. This program provides a refinancing facility for loans to the SMI sector and is open to commercial banks, some nonbank financial intermediaries and several other institutions [13]. Both the DBP and the Central Bank scheme were supported by an extension program until 1981, when its functions - mainly preparation of loan applications and project preparation - were integrated into the Small Business Advisory Centers (SBAC).

Although DBP provided medium- and long-term loans to the SMI sector earlier, new emphasis has been given to SMI customers since 1973 [14]. Loans for investment and working capital finance have a maturity of five to ten years and generally do not exceed ₱ 100,000 in the case of home-industries, ₱ 1 million in the case of small-scale industries, and ₱ 4 million in the case of medium-scale industries [15]. Interest rates of 12-14 per cent compared favorably with the maximum rate of 19 per cent applicable from 1976 to July 1981 [16]. Collateral and self-financing requirements are very moderate and priority is given to rural industries; establishments in Manila can be assisted only if they are export-oriented.

The quantitative development of the scheme is shown in Table 6-2. After relatively slow disbursements during the first two years and rather high disbursements in fiscal year 1975/76, the total amount of approved loans declined in real terms in later years. Relatively high arrears may have contributed to the sluggish development of the scheme. In fiscal year 1977/78, arrears in interest and repayment of principle amounted to about 29 per cent for small-industry loans and 28 per cent for medium-industry loans. Loans to large-scale industries, on the other hand, had arrears of less than 5 per cent of outstanding loans [17]. It is interesting to note that loans approved by the DBP headquarters have higher arrears than those approved by branch offices; this observation suggests that a more intimate knowledge of local conditions can reduce transaction costs [18].

The Industrial Guarantee and Loan Fund (IGLF) was launched in 1973 to promote lending to the SMI sector by financial institutions. Its design is quite similar to the Indonesian KIK/KMKP scheme: a combination of low-cost funds from the Central Bank, a fixed interest rate spread, and credit insurance. Loans from rural banks are limited to ₱ 20,000 - ₱ 150,000, while other institutions can disburse loans amounting to up to ₱ 0.8 million. Since 1979 medium-industry loans (₱ 0.8 - 2.5 million) were permitted to be rediscounted under the IGLF scheme. Maximum maturity is 12 years for investment credit and three years for working capital credit. Interest rates are fairly low at 12 per cent for small-industry loans (13.2 per cent since 1979) and 14 per cent for medium-industry loans [19]. Loans can be rediscounted at 7 per cent (6.7 per cent since 1979) and 9 per cent respectively. Financial institutions are left with a spread of about 5.0 - 6.5 per cent to cover administrative costs and a default risk allowance of 40 per cent for small-industry loans and 60 per cent for medium-industry loans.

In the first several years after launching the program, the response from financial institutions was quite encouraging, but in subsequent years an increasing number of institutions withdrew from the scheme (Table 6-3). In the 1976-1979 period, lending remained at a low level and recovered only in 1980 and 1981, when the interest rate spread had widened and medium-industry loans were included in the program. The changing structure of the IGLF scheme is reflected in Table 6-3. While in the first years most loans were approved by rural banks and "other" financial institutions, nonbank financial intermediaries such as the Private Development Corporation of the Philippines became the most prominent lenders in later years. In contrast to rural banks, these institutions have much experience with term lending and have a preference for larger

Table 6-2: Philippines - DBP Lending to Home, Small- and Medium-Scale Industries: Loans Approved from Fy 1973/74 to Cy 1980 (Amounts in ₱ million)

Year[a]	Home Industry Loans[b]		Small Industry Loans[b]		Medium Industry Loans[b]		Total	
	Number	Amount	Number	Amount	Number	Amount	Number	Amount
Fy 1973/74[c]	454	7.7	83	32.0	5	8.6	542	48.3
Fy 1974/75[c]	578	14.1	152	60.8	18	35.6	748	110.5
Fy 1975/76	1550	33.9	150	51.8	55	86.2	1755	171.9
Fy 1976/77	886	27.9	209	49.6	43	82.3	1138	159.8
Fy 1977/78	882	22.8	218	56.5	40	78.5	1140	157.8
Jul.-Dec. 1978	627	12.7	112	26.3	20	36.7	759	75.8
Cy 1979	786	21.4	271	65.7	48	94.0	1105	181.2
Cy 1980	789	26.0	295	77.9	48	81.7	1132	185.6
T o t a l	6552	166.5	1490	420.7	277	503.6	8319	1090.8

[a]Fy: fiscal year; Cy: calendar year. - [b]Home industry loans: up to ₱ 100,000; small industry loans: ₱ 100,000 - ₱ 1 million; medium industry loans: ₱ 1 million - ₱ 3 million. - [c]In Fy 1973/74 and 1974/75, 620 loans each under ₱ 50,000 and amounting to ₱ 8.3 million were approved by branch managers. Since their allocation between Fys is not known, they have been equally divided between Fys.

Source: Development Bank of the Philippines (DBP), unpublished.

Table 6-3: Philippines - The IGLF-Program: Loans Approved from 1973 to 1981 (Amounts in ₱ Million) by Type of Financial Institution

Year	Commercial banks			Non financial intermediaries			Other financial institutions[a]			T o t a l		
	No. of loans	Amount	No. of insti-tutions	No. of loans	Amount	No. of insti-tutions	No. of loans	Amount	No. of insti-tutions	No. of loans	Amount	No. of insti-tutions
1973	"b	"	"	"	"	"	"	"	"	8	0.3	"
1974	"	"	"	"	"	"	"	"	"	205	35.3	"
1975	69	23.9	11	-	-	-	198	22.0	81	267	45.9	92
1976	45	15.5	13	2	0.4	1	83	13.3	49	130	29.2	63
1977	19	7.7	5	26	7.5	4	26	5.1	17	71	20.3	26
1978	30	12.5	7	71	25.5	5	89	9.0	13	140	47.0	25
1979	23	11.2	5	100	42.3	4	24	6.4	8	147	59.9	17
1980	29	38.0	7	119	101.8	7	22	7.4	8	170	147.2	22
1981	28	39.5	9	170	175.0	7	24	19.9	9	222	234.4	25
Total	243	148.3	-	488	352.5	-	416	83.1	-	1360	619.5	-

[a] Includes private development banks, rural banks, savings and loan associations, and savings and mortgage banks. - b " : not available.

Source: Central Bank of the Philippines, SMILE-Department (unpublished).

clients. Thus, they can better avoid the extremely high arrears that plagued the program since its initiation [20]. Fixed interest rate spreads, as discussed above, are a major reason for financial institutions to prefer larger borrowers, i.e. lower transaction costs. In the Philippines, this behavior is reflected in a steep increase of average loan size since 1979.

The Medium- and Small-Scale Industries Coordinated Action Program (MASICAP) of 1973 did not provide financial assistance directly but rather aimed at mediating between small establishments and financial institutions by assisting small entrepreneurs in project formulation and preparation of loan applications. By June 1979, almost 6,000 projects had been evaluated, of which 4,900 had been found worthy of financial assistance and 2,500 project loans were approved. Almost 1,000 were still being processed. MASICAP-assisted projects mostly concern rural and relatively small enterprises, but arrears in 1979 of about 15 per cent of outstanding credit compared favorably with other small-scale industry projects financed by DBP and the IGLF scheme [21]. This relative success of MASICAP underlines the importance of technical assistance to banks and borrowers although the share of arrears may still not be acceptable to commercial financial institutions.

In considering financial assistance to SMIs in the Philippines, it should be noted that in 1978 financial institutions disbursed a total of ₱ 8,341 million in long-term funds to the industrial sector [22]. Compared with this figure, lending under the DBP and IGLF schemes (₱ 158 million and ₱ 48 million in the same year) was of little quantitative significance. These financial assistance programs have, however, been the most important institutional source of term loans for the SMI sector, since commercial credit was rarely available until interest rates on medium- and long-term loans were deregulated in July 1981. The programs have improved access of SMIs to institutional credit, but with respect to effectiveness of financial assistance, similar considerations apply as in the case of Indonesia. The sluggish growth of loan approvals indicates that a fixed interest rate spread and highly concessional terms do not necessarily benefit the SMI sector as a whole but tend to work in favor of credit allocation to larger, well established SMI customers.

(c)   Thailand

Financial assistance to small industrial enterprises is even less important in Thailand than in the Philippines. The only relevant program was established in 1964 and then abolished in 1980. A proposed new program has not yet been implemented. During the life span of the program that was established (17 years), only 1,181 loans to small industries, amounting to ₱ 387 million, were disbursed by the Small Industry Finance Office (SIFO), a government office under the Ministry of Industry (Table 6-4). The maximum annual number of loans was 119, in 1969 [23].

(d) Malaysia

Financial assistance to the SMI sector is not confined to specific programs in Malaysia, but is based to a significant extent on regulations and moral suasion of the Bank Negara, which intends to increase the participation of commercial banks in financing SMIs. For loans to small-scale industries (loans up to M$ 200,000), an interest rate ceiling of 10 per cent (prime rate = 8.5 per cent) was introduced in October 1976 and reduced to 9 per cent (prime rate = 7.5 per cent) in June 1977 [24]. To avoid negative repercussions on the volume of lending, as they were observed in Indonesia and the Philippines, Bank Negara has regulated credit allocation. Sixteen per cent of new loans disbursed by commercial banks must accrue to small establishments (10 per cent since 1979) [25].

Besides a number of nonbank financial institutions assisting SMIs, the one specific and important program designed to improve SMIs' access to credit from the commercial banking system is the credit insurance scheme of the Credit Guarantee Corporation (CGC). The idea behind this program is to reduce the default risk for lenders through a credit insurance scheme. For this purpose, the CGC was set up in 1973 as a joint venture of Bank Negara and commercial banks. CGC insures 60 per cent of the default risk of loans to agriculture, trade, and industry, charging 0.5 per cent of the outstanding balance. The upper limit of loans eligible for CGC coverage is M$ 100,000 (M$ 200,000 for loans to Bumiputra). The borrowing establishment may have a net worth of assets of up to M$ 100,000 (M$ 200,000 in the case of Bumiputra) [26].

In contrast to the schemes applied in Indonesia and the Philippines, there is no subsidized refinancing facility for loans to the SMI sector in Malaysia, although Bank Negara has made commercial banks' concessional lending to small establishments mandatory. Commercial banks are forced to provide a certain percentage of their savings deposits as SMI loans under CGC coverage at the fairly low interest rate of 8.5 per cent. Initially, this share was 3 per cent, but in July 1974 it was raised to 5 per cent and in July 1975 to 10 per cent. The regulated interest rate of only 8.5 per cent (effective rate 8 per cent), however, cannot compensate commercial banks for the 40 per cent of the de-

Table 6-4: Thailand - The SIFO Program: Loans Approved from
1964 to 1980 (Amounts in ฿ Million)

Fiscal Year	Loans Approved	
	Number	Amount
1964	12	2.4
1965	49	11.0
1966	70	15.7
1967	86	22.0
1968	112	26.3
1969	119	31.7
1970	114	26.4
1971	67	18.6
1972	79	21.7
1973	58	16.2
1974	43	14.9
1975	72	28.7
1976	60	26.3
1977	83	46.3
1978	85	44.8
1979	55	28.1
1980	17	6.0
Total	1181	387.1

Source: Sanguanruang et al. (1978); SIFO (unpublished).

fault risk accruing to them despite CGC coverage; banks
thus attempt to reduce transaction costs by selecting
borrowers with sufficient collateral. This practice is
revealed by the share of loans in default of which
neither principle nor interest payment can be recovered. Such loans have amounted to only 1.5 per cent in
terms of number of loans and to 0.3 per cent in terms
of loan value [27]. The interest rate ceiling thus
tends to obstruct the objective of the scheme, namely,
to support highly profitable but collateral-deficient
projects.

Table 6-5 shows that lending of commercial banks
under CGC coverage peaked in 1974 and has remained
below that level ever since. With outstanding loans at
the end of 1979 of about M$ 33 million, lending to
small-industrial enterprises under CGC remained of
fairly minor overall quantitative importance, especially when compared to the M$ 1,565 million of outstanding
commercial bank loans to total manufacturing. In 1979
only 9.3 per cent of new commercial bank loans to the
SMI sector (defined as fixed assets under M$ 500,000)
were insured by CGC [28]. The reluctance of commercial
banks to participate in the CGC scheme is also shown in
the fact that at the end of 1979 the outstanding CGC
loans amounted to only 8.5 per cent of savings deposits
thus falling short of the 10 per cent target set by
Bank Negara [29].

Table 6-5: Malaysia - Commercial Bank Credit under CGC-Cover,
1973-1980 (Approved Amounts in M$ Million)

	1973	1974	1975	1976	1977	1978	1979	1980	Total
Manufac-turing	1.1	17.7	14.8	9.9	9.5	12.8	14.0	10.0	90.7
Share of manufactur-ing in total amount (per cent)	9.3	10.8	11.8	11.1	10.7	11.1	9.8	8.8	10.5

Source: Bank Negara Malaysia, Annual Report and Statement of
Accounts. Kuala Lumpur, various issues.

While loans from commercial banks are mostly short-term, medium- and long-term funds are mainly provided by development banks such as the Malaysian Industrial Development Finance Berhad (MIDF). Loans from MIDF have a maturity of 5-15 years and can be used to finance up to 50 per cent of an investment project [30]. Small-industry loans (up to M$ 150,000) account for about two-thirds of MIDF loans in terms of number and for 11.5 per cent in terms of value. Interest rates for small-industry loans are slightly below market levels [31]. Otherwise, MIDF treats all applicants on equal terms. When SMIs have nevertheless had access to this source of finance, differences in transaction costs among establishments of different size cannot be as wide as in other ASEAN countries.

A lesser source of institutional credit is Bank Pembangunan Malaysia (BPM). Lending conditions are quite similar to those of MIDF, but loans from BPM are available only to Bumiputra entrepreneurs. Another source for Bumiputra is Majlis Amanah Rakyat (MARA); loans from MARA are on an average very small and repayment performance is considered unsatisfactory. Substantial government subsidies are necessary to finance this scheme [32].

When evaluating financial assistance to SMIs, the case of Malaysia is distinct from Indonesia or the Philippines in several respects. Subsidized credit schemes play only a marginal role in Malaysia, and the major source of SMI credit is commercial banks, which must observe interest rate ceilings. To the extent these ceilings lead to losses from SMI credits, these losses must be covered by the commercial banks themselves. The Central Bank does not offer preferential rediscount facilities, but maximum interest rates allowed for SMI credit clearly exceed the prime rate.

In light of these differences it may not be surprising that in contrast to the other countries, access to institutional credit is much less of a problem for SMIs in Malaysia. In September 1978, almost 10 per cent of total outstanding credit accrued to establishments with less than M$ 300,000 of fixed assets [33]. This allocation of credit corresponds roughly to the ratio of fixed assets between small and large establishments. Mandatory lending to SMIs imposed by Bank Negara was certainly instrumental in securing credit availability to SMIs. However, such a policy would have been hardly successful in a financial system less competitive and efficient than the Malaysian one. Competition among commercial banks forces these institutions to acknowledge SMIs as potential customers and to develop appropriate screening and loan administration procedures. Only under such conditions can commercial banks provide a substantial volume of preferential credit without subsidies from the government.

(e) Singapore

Despite the priority attached to establishing large-scale export-oriented industries, the importance of SMIs in employment creation and a sound industrial structure has not been overlooked in Singapore [34]. In a very early phase of active industrialization policies (1963) a Light Industries Services Unit (LISU) had already been set up within EDB, the national development agency of Singapore. As part of its activities, LISU provided loans to small establishments even without collateral and evaluated loan applications of SMIs submitted to commercial banks. Until 1968, when these functions were transferred to the Development Bank of Singapore (DBS), between 41 and 56 loans were disbursed per year [35].

Since the mid-1970s, financing of SMIs found renewed attention as a part of Singapore's structural adjustment policies. The Small Industries Finance Scheme (SIFS) was launched in November 1976, funded by EDB and administered by DBS. SMIs with less than S$ 1 million in fixed assets (including the project to be financed) are eligible to SIFS loans, which may amount up to S$ 600,000. The production structure of recipients should, however, be complementary to LI production, i.e., they should provide industrial services or produce components. The interest rate on SIFS loans has been fairly close to the market rate in 1976, but has declined in relative terms as it has since been kept constant at 9.5 per cent. Until April 1979, loans amounting to S$ 18.3 million had been disbursed, with an average size of about S$ 165,000 [36]. It should be noted, however, that the economic function of the SIFS scheme is quite different from financial assistance programs in other ASEAN countries; the main purpose of the SIFS scheme has not been to subsidize SMIs or to improve their access to formal credit, but to provide an additional incentive for structural adjustment in a changing economic environment. This is not surprising since SMIs' access to formal credit has not been a problem in the highly competitive financial markets in Singapore (see Chapter 5-2).

(f) Salient Features of Financial Assistance to SMIs

In Indonesia, the Philippines, and especially in Thailand, financial assistance to SMIs has remained too small in quantitative terms to offset the lack to formal credit, which is at least partly a consequence of monetary and credit policies pursued in these countries. In the comparatively liberal financial environment prevailing in Malaysia and in Singapore, access to commercial credit is much less of a problem for SMIs than in the other ASEAN countries. The small scale of specific finanical assistance for SMIs does not constitute a significant constraint to development in this sector. Access has, however, been geared by Central Bank regulations in Malaysia, although SMIs were not granted preferential interest rates vis-a-vis LIs. This example shows that concessional interest rates are not an indispensable element of SMI promotion policies. The experiences in Indonesia and the Philippines suggest that concessional terms, even if backed by refinancing schemes, may not be conducive to the goals of financing programs. Low interest ceilings and fixed interest rate spreads tend to benefit larger borrowers with sufficient collateral at the expense of economically profitable projects where little collateral can be offered. Credit insurance schemes applied in several countries have done little to prevent this bias.

The financing programs have undeniably improved the climate for SMI lending by supporting the accumulation of information and experience with respect to this kind of lending activities by both banks and SMI customers. The accumulation of experience was enhanced, however, more by technical assistance programs than through concessional financing schemes as such. The potential created by improved knowledge and information was exploited only when banks were given freedom to adjust lending terms to their perception of the risks involved. Such an approach to SMI lending does not preclude interest rate subsidies, which reduce interest rate differentials among SMI borrowers and provide access to formal credit to new and/or high risk SMI projects.

Part 2: Nonfinancial Assistance to SMIs

Despite the fact that training and advisory programs have been implemented in many countries, evaluation of their impact on the development of SMIs has been extremely limited and incomplete at best. Similarly, there is no systematic evaluation of the type of services required by SMIs at various levels of their development. Existing programs address themselves to training entrepreneurs and workers, to procurement and marketing problems, and, in rare cases, to infrastructural bottlenecks. The following section will be confined to a review of the quantitative significance of such programs and will offer some ex ante considerations on the nature and goals of nonfinancial assistance to SMIs.

Programs of nonfinancial assistance to SMIs are intended to tackle constraints that are generally believed to reduce efficiency. Among such constraints are a lack of technical and market information, deficient accounting and management practices, and a lack of entrepreneurial ability. Since the supply of respective services on a commercial basis is regarded as insufficient or beyond the reach of SMIs, it is concluded that such services must be provided by publicly financed schemes more or less free of charge. In ASEAN countries, however, only a small minority of SMIs has been reached by the respective programs.

In Indonesia the most important extension program is BIPIK (Guidance and Development of Small Industry). BIPIK is a very ambitious program. It is not only intended to give advice to SMIs, but also to offer training of workers and entrepreneurs, to assist SMIs in the procurement of raw materials and in marketing their products, and to centrally provide certain types of equipment in "mini-estates" [37]. At present, however, financial and manpower resources are still rather limited. In early 1980, BIPIK had a staff of only 150 - 200, much of which was on a part-time basis. Only a tiny fraction of the target population could be reached.

Similar half-hearted approaches have been adopted in the Philippines and Thailand. In the Philippines, Small Business Advisory Centers (SBAC) have been set up throughout the country starting in 1974. By June 1979, 1,065 new or existing establishments had received assistance free of charge [38]. In Thailand extension and training services are available from the Division of Industrial Services (DIS), which was founded in 1966 under the heading Small Industry Service Institute (SISI). SISI started its activities in Bangkok in 1968 and opened a regional office in Chiengmai in 1972. Sanguanruang et al. found in a sample survey that a majority of SMIs had never even heard of SISI/DIS and that only 8.7 per cent of them had even been clients [39]. One of the biggest problems of DIS is the high rate of staff turnover; as a government agency DIS cannot offer sufficiently attractive salaries.

In Malaysia there are several agencies providing nonfinancial assistance to SMIs. Only Bumiputra entrepreneurs have access to the Advisory Services Development Division of MARA, but according to Chee et al., a lack of qualified personnel limited both the quality and the quantity of assistance [40]. In contrast to MARA, all SMI enterprises have access to the services provided by MIDF Industrial Consultant (MIDFIC). MIDFIC has specialized in the preparation of feasibility studies and in the analysis of marketing problems. Its quantitative impact remains limited though; the quantitative importance of assistance provided by other agencies is even lesser [41]. The sample survey conducted by Chee et al. shows that just eight out of 239 SMIs questioned had received advice from one of the relevant agencies. The main sources of information and advice available to SMIs were other businessmen, partners, suppliers, friends, and family members [42].

In Singapore publicly funded extension services for SMIs had become largely redundant in the early 1970s, when full employment of the labor force was achieved and a broad range of commercial services became available. The Light Industries Services Unit of EDB was abolished in 1973. In recent years, however, a Product Development Assistance Scheme (PDAS) has been established to support local entrepreneurs in upgrading their operations.

The scope of nonfinancial assistance to SMIs in ASEAN countries has been quite limited. An evaluation of its effectiveness in upgrading SMIs is prevented by the lack of respective data, but a few general considerations can be offered. One issue is that, in general, services are provided free of charge, even if the programs directly compete with services supplied by the private sector. Although it may be somewhat unrealistic to demand cost reflecting fees for extension services, sufficient attention should be paid to the side-effects of such programs on the desired development of a private supply of business services. Government programs should aim at supplementing commercially available services rather than offering substitutes.

A second issue is that technical and marketing services typically require a highly specialized knowledge of the respective industry. It is questionable whether government agencies have a comparative advantage in providing such services. Alternative and possibly more adequate sources of specialized services are entities such as industrial associations. Development of such associations may itself be a highly rewarding program; service centers could then focus on the functions of problem identification and referral to competent advisors.

Concerning the issue of infrastructural requirements, two quite contradictory views can be found in the literature. On one hand, it is argued that SMIs are much less demanding in this respect than LIs and hence can be easily dispersed regionally. On the other hand, it can be argued that nontraditional SMIs need an assured supply of public utilities and services in areas such as transportation, communication, business advice, and trading. SMIs cannot provide such services themselves because of the sizeable fixed cost element involved. As has already been stated by Staley and Morse [43], the first argument seems to apply only to traditional establishments that have always been regionally dispersed, while the latter argument provides some clues with respect to possible bottlenecks for the development of nontraditional SMIs. One example of this is the supply of electricity. Usually, an adequate supply of electricity is only available in the larger towns; in rural areas in Indonesia, Thailand, and the Philippines, electricity supply is still rudimentary and unreliable. Supply of electrical energy, however, is essential for nontraditional SMIs in many industries [44]. Industrial estates could potentially be an adequate means of providing such infrastructural facilities in an efficient way, but at present, industrial estates do not play a significant role as a location for SMIs in ASEAN countries [45].

Part 3: Lessons from the Policy Analysis

The preceding analysis of industrialization policies in ASEAN countries has established the significance of macroeconomic policies for SMI development (Chapter 5). Foreign trade and investment promotion policies create constraints to profitability and growth of SMIs to the extent that second-stage import substitution is emphasized and selective measures proliferate. The situation is aggravated for SMIs if highly interventionistic credit policies impede rather than improve access to formal sources of finance. SMI promotion policies have not been able to offset biases in favor of large establishments inherent in such macroeconomic policies. Both financial and nonfinancial assistance has undoubtedly supported SMI development, but assistance was neither sufficient in quantitative terms nor appropriate in terms of design.

The obvious conclusion from these findings is that policy changes are required, particularly in those countries where the economic environment is strongly biased against SMI development. Such policy changes can concern the volume and design of government assistance to SMIs as well as industrialization policies themselves. Both options and their relationship to each other, based on an evaluation of bottlenecks SMIs are facing in their development process (Chapter 7) will be considered in subsequent Chapter 8.

NOTES

1. For an overview see Arief (1981) and Bolnick (1982).

2. Previously Rp. 20 million, assuming average investment cost of US-$ 3,000 per worker, the limit of US-$ 160,000 excludes many MIs.

3. For a detailed description of lending conditions see Arief (1981). Clients who have grown beyond KIK/KMKP limits can apply for Kredit Kelayakan (Feasibility Credit).

4. See Arief (1981).

94

5. To compute growth rates in real terms, the wholesale price index, excluding exports, was used.

6. Arrears in interest payment and repayment of principal amounted to about 20 per cent of outstanding loans on March 31, 1981. Because of the newness of the program involving medium-term loans, this figure should be considered carefully. See Arief (1981, p. 20).

7. See Hill (1979, pp. 205 ff.).

8. See Bruch (1982b, p. 23).

9. See Arief (1981, pp. 21 ff.).

10. See e.g. Arief (1981, pp. 10 f.).

11. Concessional credit for LIs was available at an interest rate of about 12-15 per cent. See Hill (1979, p. 194).

12. See Anderson (1982, pp. 49 ff.).

13. For cottage industries there are two other sources of subsidized credit, the National Cottage Industries Authority (NACIDA) and the recently established Kilusan Kaunlaran at Kabuhayan (KKK) scheme.

14. According to the definition applied by DBP, home industries have fixed assets of less than ₱ 100,000, small-scale industries of ₱ 100,000 - ₱ 1 million, and medium-scale industries of ₱ 1 million - ₱ 4 million. These limits were substantially raised in 1981.

15. Since 1980 the following limits apply: home industry loans up to ₱ 170,000, SI loans ₱ 170,000 - ₱ 1.7 million, MI loans ₱ 1.7 million - ₱ 5 million.

16. Lending conditions have, however, been under revision in early 1982.

17. See Anderson, Khambata (1981, pp. 181 f.).

18. Ibid (1981, p. 25).

19. An administrative charge of up to 1.5 per cent p.a. is added to interest payments.

20. In September 1978 arrears amounted to 34.2 per cent of outstanding credit, according to a sample survey of commercial banks by Anderson and Khambata (1981, p. 18).

21. See MASICAP (1979).

22. See World Bank (1980, p. 33). It should be noted that it is a common practice in the Philippines to roll over short-term credit. This practice, however, is usually confined to larger clients.

23. For further details as well as lending conditions see Sanguanruang et al. (1978, pp. 131 ff.).

24. See Bank Negara Malaysia (1979, pp. 131 f., 371 f.).

25. For further quantitative controls see Bank Negara Malaysia (1979, pp. 133, 166 ff.).

26. See Chee, Puthucheary, Lee (1979, p. 35).

27. See Bank Negara Malaysia (Annual Report 1979, pp. 72 ff.).

28. Bank Negara Malaysia (Annual Report 1979, pp. 72 ff.).

29. Bank Negara Malaysia (Annual Report 1979, pp. 72 ff.).

30. Only components of the project itself are used as collateral.

31. See Bank Negara Malaysia (1979, pp. 211 f.).

32. See Chee, Foong (1979) and Chee, Puthucheary, Lee (1979) for details.

33. See Bank Negara Malaysia (1979, pp. 166 f.).

34. See Economic Development Board (1962, p. 3).

35. In 1967 LISU loans amounted to only about 0.6 per cent of loans outstanding to manufacturing.

36. See Economic Development Board (1978/79, p. 20).

37. See International Development Center of Japan (1977/78, pp. 27 ff.).

38. See Anderson, Khambata (1981, pp. 52 ff. 197). Information on a number of other agencies as well as on "entrepreneurial development programs" is contained in U.P. Institute for Small-Scale Industries (1979).

39. See Sanguanruang et al. (1978, pp. 127, 161 ff.).

40. For details see Chee, Puthucheary, Lee (1979).

41. Ibid (1979).

42. Ibid (1979, pp. 124 ff.).

43. See Staley, Morse (1965, pp. 304 ff.).

44. See Minami (1976).

45. See Bruch (1982c).

7
Impediments to SMI Development: A Micro View

Part 1:   Basic Impediments as Perceived by SMIs

The policy analysis presented in Chapters 5 and 6 has provided evidence of policy-induced discrimination of SMIs in most ASEAN countries which explains at least in part the poor performance of SMIs discussed in Sections 2.2. and 3.3. Discrimination vis-a-vis larger establishments is felt by SMIs in various ways, such as limited access to formal credit, high input cost, lack of skilled workers, etc. Many of these consequences of macroeconomic and sector policies are interrelated and mutually reinforcing. Policy recommendations require an understanding of the true causal relationships to pinpoint the areas in which policy changes are needed most urgently to remove bottlenecks for SMI development. This section presents an overview of the most salient problems SMI entrepreneurs envisage when setting up, expanding, or simply running their businesses. Impediments as they are perceived by individual entrepreneurs do not necessarily indicate the true causes for low levels of economic efficiency in SMIs, but they provide a convenient starting point for an analysis of common bottlenecks for SMI development.

The nature and the relative importance of perceived impediments varies among different types of SMIs (rural - urban, traditional - nontraditional, etc.), with the type of market served (local or domestic final demand, intermediate demand, export markets), and with the economic environment. In general, however, financing of working capital needs emerged as the most frequently mentioned problem area in several sample surveys conducted in different countries [1]. Other frequently mentioned problem areas were the procurement of raw materials, stiff competition and slack demand, and problems with labor, land and buildings.

Evidence from various sources shows that the lack of working capital is mainly a blend of problems related to obtaining loans from financial institutions, pressure to extend credit to customers, collection of trade debts, and shortages of internal funds as a result of low profitability [2]. New and expanding enterprises are particularly prone to problems with financing working capital. Frequently, existing collateral has been used up to receive loans for the purchase of fixed assets while new customers may be unreliable or may have to be gained by extending credit.

Supply of raw materials and intermediate inputs of the required specifications is often unstable in quality, quantity, and price because of deficiencies in the trade sector and lack of infrastructure in transportation and communication. LIs, on the other hand, can rely on long-term contracts and favorable prices for bulk purchases.

Problems related to competition and marketing are manifold. Competition seems to be especially stiff in markets for simple standardized items where technological and capital requirements are low. Often, innovations in product design are immediately imitated by competitors, but readily available information on product markets is scarce in most cases, and SMIs are often surprised by changes in the structure of demand. Such a relatively high degree of instability, both in output and input markets, may result in low degrees of capacity utilization and thus low profitability and inefficient factor use.

Among the problems related to labor, a lack of skilled workers seems to be felt, especially among modern SMIs that find it difficult to compete with LIs. SMIs also complain about LIs bidding away workers after a significant amount of training has been invested. Besides higher wages, aspects of job security, a more pleasant work place and a higher status value are reasons for the workers' preferences for employment in LIs.

Another important problem affecting SMIs relates to the site of their operations. Many SMIs are operating in congested residential areas, but their business premises are often poorly laid out and many man-hours are lost in unproductive activities. SMIs frequently depend on rented workshops or factory buildings and must worry about increases in rent and renewal of leases. SMIs located in rural areas complain about insufficient supply of energy and severe bottlenecks in the transportation sector that affect both the availability of inputs and the distribution of output.

The individual problems perceived by SMIs are to some extent interrelated. A few examples illustrate this issue. A lack of working capital, for example, may lead to insufficient stocks of raw materials and spare parts. Chee found a number of cases in his 1973 sample survey of SMIs in Malaysia in which production had to be interrupted and workers laid off because materials could not be paid for [3]. Lack of access to formal investment finance may preclude the purchase of equipment needed to upgrade product quality and gain access to more lucrative markets. On the other hand, it is likely that a low level of profitability will make it difficult for an establishment to gain access to formal finance.

There are several problems likely to be more severe in some markets than in others. In a study on subcontracting in the Filipino automobile industry, Watanabe found that the small domestic market for the final product combined with substantial market segmentation had resulted in small and sporadic jobs for subcontractors [4]. This situation was aggravated by the practice of LIs playing subcontractors off against each other in order to reduce prices. Because of the sporadic nature of orders, there is little advantage in economies of scale. Specialized equipment does not pay off, and product quality is poor. Other complaints of subcontractors were occasional shortages of materials, poor and irregular quality of materials, speculation and hoarding by merchants, and tedious import procedures. Problems of work scheduling and a lack of working capital often led to delays in delivery. Thus, purchases of LIs from local subcontractors were found to be largely limited to a small amount of low-technology items [5].

In export markets, there are a number of problems also pertinent to LIs but which seem to be much more difficult for SMIs to overcome. These include, inter alia, a lack of information about international trading practices, insufficient knowledge of the patterns of demand and supply in foreign markets, deficiencies in the quality of products, difficulties in meeting dates of delivery, and the need to cope with administrative procedures. Many of these problems are more pertinent to SMIs than to LIs for the simple reason that selling abroad involves higher fixed cost than selling at home. In a discriminant analysis of the characteristics of small-scale exporters versus nonexporters among manufacturing establishments in Malaysia, it was found that lack of working capital and problems with the procurement of raw materials rank high in precluding many SMIs from entering export markets [6]. Working capital requirements are typically relatively high in exporting activities because of a longer period between shipment and receipt of payment. A good and reliable supply of raw materials is also essential for exporting because of higher quality standards and punctuality requirements.

Part 2: The Surface and Below

(a) Determinants of Economic Performance:
    Internal Causes

Two sets of causes for the above mentioned problems of SMIs can be identified. The first relates to the question of why some SMIs perform better than others under the same external conditions; the second set relates to the question of why there are differences in the average performance of SMIs among countries.

The problems described in the preceding section are a reflection of market imperfections such as market segmentation, oligopolistic competition in input and output markets, or increased uncertainty for SMI decision-making. For accidental reasons, some SMIs may be in a better position to tackle these problems than others, but basically all face the same environment, at least ex ante. Several studies show, however, that establishments with widely differing levels of profitability and economic efficiency coexist in the same market [7].

Coping with market imperfections can be regarded as one of the main entrepreneurial functions [8]. In a situation where markets are fragmented, inputs are not readily available, and information is scarce or unreliable, an entrepreneur must invest a significant amount of innovative energy to be successful. This does not imply that the problems of SMIs in financing capital needs, in managing inputs and reaching product markets, and in procuring business services and information can be completely removed by an entrepreneur even if his capabilities are outstanding. Yet, market imperfections also create a spectrum of opportunities of which a good entrepreneur can take advantage.

The quality of management and entrepreneurship is revealed as the most important determinant of economic performance of SMIs in a number of micro-level studies. An analysis of major causes for arrears in MASICAP assisted projects shows that demand was overestimated in investment decisions, and working capital requirements were underestimated [9]. Another common management deficiency of SMIs in developing countries is the lack of appropriate accounting as a base for control of current operations and planning. Ho reports that fewer than one-third of establishments in Korea with 20-49 workers practice double-entry bookkeeping and fewer than one-half have any recognizable form of bookkeeping at all [10]. A similar situation has been found for the Philippines [11]. In a study of the wood and furniture industries in Ghana, Page attempted to identify variables that might explain why production costs of some firms are significantly higher than of others [12]. He concluded that variations in managerial effort and ability are significant factors in explaining a firm's position relative to the industry production frontier [13]. A recent study on Colombian SMIs by Cortes and Ishaq supports this conclusion and provides more detail with respect to the type of entrepreneur who is successful [14]. Cortes and Ishaq found that previous experience of the entrepreneur is an important determinant of the firm's performance. It was found that in the mechanical sector, skilled workers who have come to establish their own firms (usually small ones) do worse than entrepreneurs with management experience. The level of entrepreneur's formal education did, however, not appear to be a significant factor in a firm's efficiency [15].

A seldom-applied approach is the analysis of the causes leading to a firm's failure. Failure rates are typically high for newly established small businesses. Itao found in the Philippines that the average life span of bankrupt SMIs in manufacturing was three years [16] and concluded that "the primary cause of failure among small firms can be collectively attributed to management weaknesses. More specifically, these include lack of accounting records and nonhiring of a CPA/ bookkeeper" [17]. Related evidence emerges from a regression analysis of the determinants of capacity utilization in Malaysian SMIs [18]. This analysis shows that previous experience of the entrepreneur and - contrary to Cortes/Ishaq's findings - his formal education have a significantly positive impact on capacity utilization levels [19].

It has been argued that access to formal credit for investment finance as well as for financing of working capital is an important determinant of economic performance in nontraditional SMIs. Such access, however, depends not only on credit policies but also on the characteristics of an establishment and its entrepreneur. This was shown in a discriminant analysis for Malaysian SMIs [20]. According to this analysis, access to formal credit not only increases with the size and age of an establishment, but also with experience and vocational training of the entrepreneur. Other business interests of the entrepreneur and knowledge of institutional support for SMIs (as a proxy for general awareness of the economic environment) also prove to be helpful in obtaining formal credit [21].

(b) Determinants of Economic Performance:
     External Causes

While entrepreneurial and managerial quality are
the most important determinants of differing levels of
profitability and efficiency in factor use between
individual SMIs in more or less the same economic environment, there are also influences beyond the control
of the individual SMI. Such influences arise from economic policies and programs as well as from the institutional and infrastructural environment [22]. In a
situation where monetary and credit policies as well as
a low level of financial development are barriers to
SMIs' access to formal credit, entrepreneurs are largely confined to own funds and informal sources of credit, such as family members, friends, moneylenders, and
suppliers. Funds available through these sources are
likely to be inadequate and their availability uncertain. Informal loans also tend to have relatively short
maturities.

A sufficient and reliable supply of funds for
financing working capital is, however, a necessary
condition for production processes being sufficiently
smooth. This is particularly true in the case of establishments trying to upgrade and expand their operations. When problems with the supply of working capital
are anticipated and a relatively low and fluctuating
rate of capacity utilization is expected, entrepreneurs
tend to make use of relatively simple and labor-
intensive techniques of production in order to avoid
high overhead costs. Such techniques may restrict SMIs
to the production of low quality products, precluding
entry to more profitable markets. This may also explain
why the availability of funds for the purchase of
equipment and other fixed assets is less frequently
regarded as a major problem by SMI entrepreneurs; many
are more concerned with daily survival than with
upgrading and expanding operations.

The latter can be regarded as being largely due to
discrimination against SMIs by foreign trade and investment promotion policies. In general, SMIs are put
at a disadvantage by relatively low or negative EPRs
while LIs pay lower prices for imported capital goods
and materials and receive higher prices for their products as a result of selective tariffs, exemptions from
import duties, and export incentives. The establishment
size bias in the structure of effective incentive rates
tends to be even more pronounced because of tax incentives and preferential treatment of LIs with respect to
provision of public utilities. Such discrimination not
only has direct effects on the economic performance of
SMIs, but also has indirect effects, first, by depressing demand for SMI products, secondly, by limiting the
ability of SMIs to upgrade and become more active in

markets for intermediate products and in export markets, and thirdly, by causing negative repercussions on institutional infrastructure and the supply of business services. The first two issues were discussed in detail in Chapter 5; the third requires further elaboration.

It should be noted that a firm's operations include not only production in a technical sense, but also activities such as product development and design, quality control, collecting information on input and product markets, keeping stocks of materials and spare parts, equipment maintenance, and marketing, as well as dealing with organizational, legal, and fiscal matters. Common characteristics of such activities are a relatively high fixed cost element and the fact that these factors can either be produced within the firm or bought from outside. Because of the fixed cost element involved, SMIs depend to a much larger extent on an external supply of such services than do LIs. In many developing countries, however, the external supply of business services is deficient, and decision-making in SMIs takes place under increased uncertainty compared to LIs. This situation results in the use of simple equipment [23], in low levels of capacity utilization, and in lower chances of succeeding as subcontractors and in export markets because of low product quality and lack of reliability.

On the other hand, a likely reason for the deficient supply of the respective services is a lack of effective demand because of low levels of profitability on the side of potential SMI clients. This, in turn, can be regarded as a consequence of discrimination against SMIs by economic policies. In Singapore, where policy-induced discrimination against SMIs is negligible, the external supply of such services is comparatively good. This may explain why in this country SIs and MIs are efficient in industries, in which in Malaysia and the Philippines only MIs or LIs are efficient (Chapter 3.3).

In considering external influences, it can be concluded that discrimination against SMIs is likely to lead to a low-level equilibrium trap. Depressed demand for SMI products, a high degree of competition because of low barriers to entry, low levels of profitability and lack of access to formal finance may effectively preclude any upgrading of the businesses which would be a prerequisite to the survival of SMIs in an industrializing economy. The requirements of day-to-day survival are absorbing all entrepreneurial energy.

Similar arguments apply to the market for intermediate products and to export markets. In many countries trade barriers have led to foreign direct investment of a defensive nature and thus to highly segmented markets, especially for consumer durables such as automobiles. As Watanabe [24] has shown for the Philippines, this, in turn, creates low and irregular demand for subcontracting services. Investment in specialized equipment and quality control does not show an adequate return. Discrimination against SMIs in export markets through the structure of EPRs and by the nonavailability of export incentives is reflected in a lack of export services and trading houses. Such services are essential for SMIs to become more important contributors to foreign exchange earnings. In Hong Kong, the export success of SMIs has been supported by a proliferation of import-export houses. A business survey shows that 45 per cent of SMIs obtained orders solely from such trading houses [25]. Similarly, the export success of Filipino cottage products is largely due to export marketing by NACIDA [26]. In Colombia, similar evidence has been brought forward by Cortes and Ishaq, who showed that benefit-cost ratios were better for establishments with access to large distributors [27].

NOTES

1. See Chee (1975, p. 341); Chee, Puthucheary, Lee (1979, pp. 122 ff.); UPISSI (1979, pp. 27 ff.); Sharma (1979, pp. 233 ff.).
2. See e.g. Chee (1975, pp. 340 ff.).
3. See Chee (1975, pp. 340 ff.).
4. See Watanabe (1979).
5. Ibid (1979, p. 56).
6. See Bruch (1980).
7. See e.g. Cortes, Ishaq (1981).
8. See Leibenstein (1968, pp. 39 ff.).
9. See MASICAP (1979).
10. See Ho (1980, p. 83).
11. See Anderson (1982, p. 40).
12. See Page (1980).
13. Ibid (1980, p. 335).
14. See Cortes, Ishaq (1981).
15. Cortes, Ishaq (1981, p. 7).
16. See Itao (1980).
17. Ibid (1980, p. iii). CPA: Certified Public Accountant.
18. See Bruch (1982c, Ch. 5).
19. Significantly positive regression coefficients were also found for the plant size and capital intensity variables as well as for an agglomeration dummy.
20. See Bruch (1982c, Ch. 4).
21. It must be recalled, however, that financial repression is relatively mild in Malaysia.

22. Internal and external determinants of economic performance on the microeconomic level become inter-related when the supply of entrepreneurs and entre-preneurial qualities are regarded as a function of the evironment. This issue, however, is beyond the scope of the present study. Relevant references are Anderson (1982) and Roepke (1979) as well as the literature cited there.

23. For a production function analysis of this issue see Bruch (1982c, Ch. 5).

24. Watanabe (1979).

25. See Sit, Wong, Kiang (1979, p. 405).

26. See NACIDA (undated).

27. See Cortes, Ishaq (1981, p. 8).

8
Mobilizing the Development Potential of SMIs

Part 1: Policy Objectives

Turning from diagnosis to cure, the scope for appropriate government intervention comes into focus. Government action and public institutions cannot serve as panacea for all deficiencies in the functioning of private enterprises or markets, and attempts of governments to take over certain functions usually performed by the private sector have seldom led to smoother development of the economy, but rather discouraged or even prevented efficient operations.

One severe limitation to government cures is that SMI entrepreneurs lack innovativeness. Extension services may be successful in providing entrepreneurs with additional knowledge about technology, bookkeeping, marketing, etc., but such services can hardly create innovative talent [1]. This talent emerges from a complex system of social, cultural and ethical factors that can hardly be influenced by government policies in the short- or medium-run. What policy makers can do, however, is to create an economic environment in which private initiative and ingenuity is rewarded, thus encouraging actual and potential entrepreneurs to use their talent in an optimal way.

Designing an appropriate framework in which economically viable SMIs can flourish rather than intervening in the functioning of enterprises or markets should be the general guideline of any SMI promotion policy. Government institutions should not seek to assist existing SMIs or create such enterprises in specific subsectors or regions supposedly suited to SMI development. Private entrepreneurs detect much easier than bureaucrats the unmet needs of consumers and potential markets for small suppliers. Experience proves that SMIs emerge in almost any sector in any country independent of economic policies. SMIs also tend to disappear rapidly, though; a high rate of failure is, however, not necessarily a sign of lacking support to SMIs but may reflect the selection process taking place in any dynamic economy. The analysis provided in Chapter 3 has shown that SMIs are technically as well as economically inefficient in a number of industries, and SMI promotion policies should not prevent uneconomic activities from dropping out of the picture. The objective of such policies should instead be to encourage unbiased competition between small and large enterprises as well as among small enterprises themselves.

The design of such appropriate policies has been subject to a lively debate. Although the possibility of unfavorable effects of macroeconomic policies of SMI development is no longer denied, most of the literature on SMIs has focused on specific promotion measures in financial and other fields. It is explicitly or implicitly argued that the macroeconomic environment must be considered as given and unchangeable in a relevant period of time. Disadvantages that SMIs are facing would have to be diminished by specific, mostly concessional government intervention in favor of SMIs. This view has served as rationale for the SMI promotion policies in many countries.

An opposite view is taken by those who attach less weight to political rigidities that may prevent changes of macroeconomic and sector policies. According to this school of thought, an appropriate reorientation of general industrialization policies would be sufficient to activate the development potential of SMIs. It is argued that direct intervention in favor of SMIs is not required and may rather cause additional distortions in resource allocation.

The merits and shortfalls of these two approaches to SMI development will be briefly discussed in subsequent sections. A priori considerations suggest, however, that both approaches neglect important aspects of reality. The first underestimates the scope for changes in macroeconomic policies, as apparent from the policy response to pressing balance-of-payments and employment problems that have taken place in ASEAN countries in recent years; the second disregards the possibility of institutional rigidities and market imperfections that would not simply disappear as a result of liberal trade, investment and credit policies. Therefore, a third approach is presented in Part 4, focusing on gradual changes in the macroeconomic framework combined with appropriate measures to support SMI development.

Part 2: The Traditional Approach

According to the traditional approach financial assistance, extension services, marketing assistance, and the provision of infrastructural facilities are considered as necessary and sufficient elements in a government intervention package intending to diminish

policy-induced disadvantages of SMIs and to ease constraints to their contribution to output and employment
growth [2]. This approach has provided the rationale
for SMI promotion policies applied in ASEAN countries
and elsewhere. It would be unreasonable to deny any
positive effect of such measures. Financial assistance
has improved the access of SMIs to formal credit in all
ASEAN countries that have applied such a policy. Equally, extension services have been valuable sources of
advice for those SMIs assisted. Although neglected to
date, marketing assistance such as the promotion of
subcontracting arrangements and assistance in export
marketing may also be helpful in reducing specific
problems of SMIs [3]. Similarly, SMIs are able to benefit from infrastructural facilities adjusted to their
needs.

These improvements, however, do not necessarily
justify the respective policy measures in economic
terms. The resources used for promotion of SMIs might
have produced more output and employment elsewhere in
the economy. Unfortunately, there is no information to
quantify the actual or potential social efficiency of
this policy, but some of its features give reasons for
severe doubts.

The programs actually implemented have so far
failed to generate impact of any quantitative significance, frequently they have created additional distortions and have suffered from a number of internal
inconsistencies reducing their effectiveness. While
some of these shortcomings may be cured by modifying
the design of the respective programs or by increasing
resource commitments, there are fundamental considerations leading to the conclusion that the results of
specific assistance to SMIs may remain unsatisfactory
as long as the plant size bias in the general policy
framework is not substantially reduced.

It is important to note that negative repercussions
from macroeconomic and sectoral policies would have to
be compensated for by direct or client-focussed measures. While such intervention may not pose a major
problem with respect to a small number of LIs, as exem-
plified by export promotion measures, a significant
amount of financial resources and adequately trained
manpower would be required to do the same for the vast
number of SMIs, not to mention CIs. In addition, an
effective promotion policy must be based on an integrated approach simultaneously attacking the multiple
problems of SMIs in areas such as financing, marketing,
and management. Given these requirements, it can be
easily seen that a complete package compensating SMIs
for policy-induced disadvantages is beyond the means of
any developing country and would hardly be efficient
compared to alternative use of the financial and administrative resources involved.

Aside from resource requirements, SMI promotion policies create new problems and do not always successfully tackle the true causes of sluggish SMI development. An example concerning the first point is the changing relationship between governments and entrepreneurs when preferential treatment is offered. On the side of the governments, it may prove difficult to prevent abuses of power when selecting candidates for government assistance. With respect to entrepreneurs, efforts to obtain preferential treatment may become more rewarding than genuinely entrepreneurial activities.

Concerning the second point, it should be recalled that second-stage import substitution policies tend to depress final demand for SMI products and discriminate against SMIs as suppliers of intermediate products and as exporters. Such an economic environment makes it much more difficult and costly to obtain a quantitatively significant result from SMI promotion than under a less biased policy framework. Promotion measures tend to be less efficient because a higher degree of resistance on the demand side has to be overcome. This is reflected in several problems that plague SMI promotion programs in ASEAN countries. In general, demand for assistance, even at concessional terms, has been found to be relatively sluggish. The often deplored lack of profitable investment projects suitable for SMIs cannot, however, be ascribed to a lack of entrepreneurs, since the entrepreneurial response to market opportunities is in general highly elastic [4]. Apparently, demand for investment finance as well as for services or infrastructure suited to nontraditional SMIs is relatively low when demand for the products of such enterprises is adversely affected by economic policies. One typical example is the industrial estate in Rungkut, Surabaya (Indonesia), which had initially been designed to accomodate SMIs, but had to be redesigned because of a lack of SMIs responding.

The degree of difficulty in escaping from the low-level equilibrium trap mentioned above is illustrated by the high level of arrears in lending to SMIs under various credit schemes, especially in Indonesia and the Philippines. Often production costs are underestimated. As a consequence, cash flow is low and shortages of working capital occur. A survey of MASICAP-assisted projects in the Philippines, for example, has shown that 55 per cent of accounts in arrears resulted from financial and marketing problems [5]. These findings support the conclusion that assistance to SMIs can only marginally improve the prospects of SMI development when the current discrimination by the policy framework is not gradually eliminated.

Part 3: The Neo-Liberal Approach

The preceding analysis leads to the conclusion that deregulation of financial markets, reform of foreign trade policies and review of investment promotion measures are necessary preconditions for a significantly enhanced contribution of SMIs to employment, output, and income generation. But would the removal of the plant size bias from macroeconomic and sectoral policies also be sufficient to mobilize the development potential of SMIs ? It has been argued that specific measures to assist a certain group of establishments (or any other group of economic entities) are undesirable per se since such measures would only introduce new distortions into the system of incentives [6]. Any rationale for specific measures is denied on the grounds that market forces have proven to be the superior mechanism in securing an efficient allocation of resources and in bringing about the necessary institutional environment (in particular financial institutions).

Adoption of this approach would require governments of ASEAN countries to substantially review their industrialization policies. An analysis of monetary and credit policies in these countries (Chapter 5.2) shows that in order to remove the plant size bias in financial markets, the functions of central banks would have to be reduced to control of monetary aggregates, to provide "lender of last resort" services and generally supervise financial institutions. This implies equal refinancing conditions for all financial institutions, abolishment of specific credit ceilings and deregulation of interest rates both for lending operations and deposits. In such a framework, financial institutions would be free of differentiate among borrowers according to transaction costs and SMIs would compete for funds with other borrowers on equal terms. Financial liberalization would also be expected to enhance the development of financial markets. SMIs would be able to benefit from both better performance of financial institutions and from a higher competition among financial institutions.

Improved access to formal credit would facilitate financing of both fixed assets and working capital. New profitable investment opportunities for SMIs would be created when selective measures in foreign trade and investment promotion policies were abolished. Such a reorientation of policies concerns such measures as foreign exchange and import controls, tariff protection on a case-by-case basis, exemptions from import duties and corporate income taxes, and subsidized export credit, all of which have been found to discriminate directly against the SMI-sector in ASEAN countries (Chapter 5.1). In a further step, the level and structure of import tariffs would have to be reviewed in order to achieve lower and uniform rates of tariff protection.

Such a reform of trade and investment policies is expected to increase domestic final demand for SMI products and to eliminate the discrimination against SMI exports, thus opening new possibilities for existing SMIs and for the establishment of new enterprises. Similarly, domestic demand for intermediate products is likely to expand and encourage closer cooperation among both smaller and larger enterprises.

It cannot be denied, that eliminating biases from macroeconomic policies has merits for labor-absorbing industrial development in general [7] and for the development of SMIs in particular. This ideal long-run solution does, however, not take into account a number of limitations resulting from imperfections of the real world. The experience of Singapore, where the performance of SMIs was similar to mostly foreign-owned large-scale enterprises in the 1970s, is not easily transferable to other countries. In Singapore, government intervention into economic activities was designed at the onset to minimize policy-induced price distortions and to encourage international competition in all sectors of the economy, including the financial sector. Without entering into a discussion of whether such a strategy may be viable for other countries as well, it can be stated that the other ASEAN countries had opted for a more inward-oriented approach to economic development in the 1960s and that most of them have begun to gradually liberalize their systems of economic incentives only recently. This change of emphasis in development policies has created a need for structural adjustment in all sectors of the economy.

Adjustment of economic activities to match changing macroeconomic parameters, however, takes place neither instantaneously nor free of charge. Economic liberalization forces industrial enterprises to change their output composition, upgrade production processes, explore new markets and, above all, invest in new equipment. Financial institutions have to begin a process of reorientation and adjustment as a result of increasing competition in financial markets. The supply of specialized industrial services required by SMIs in particular does not develop quickly, and adjustment of the supply of infrastructural facilities to the new economic environment takes considerable time. For such reasons, the transition period may be lengthy and full of friction, which will impede employment and output growth [8]. Friction as well as externalities associated with economic adjustment seem to warrant supportive measures, which facilitate and shorten the transition period. This approach to SMI promotion policies is suggested by this study.

Part 4: A Piecemeal Approach

The policy conclusions derived in this section are based on the commitment of the governments of ASEAN countries to maintain or improve the level of international competitiveness of their economies. Countries pursuing more inward-oriented development strategies in the past have begun to open up their markets to international competition and this progress is envisaged to continue gradually, including at least some deregulation of financial markets. These policy changes tend to improve the economic environment of SMIs but also create adjustment problems, which justify appropriately designed SMI promotion measures.

The design of specific measures to support structural adjustment in the SMI sector must be based on a clear understanding of what such measures are to achieve. The reduction or eventual elimination of the plant size bias in the policy framework creates a potential for existing SMIs to upgrade or expand their operations and for new enterprises to be established [9]. Potential value added in the SMI sector will increase as depicted by line AA in Figure 8-1.

Figure 8-1

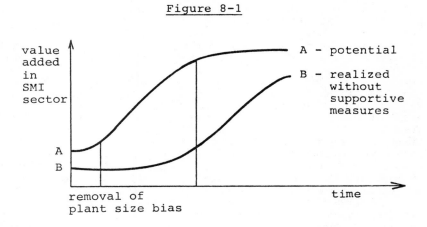

Without supportive measures, such potential may be realized only in the long run (line BB in Figure 8-1) because of lagging factors both internal and external to an establishment. The level and sophistication of management practices may change only slowly in the transition from traditional to nontraditional activities or when the firm is growing and operations are becoming more complicated. Similarly, new establishments are prone to high failure rates because of a lack of experience. The average level of X-efficiency can be expected to decline temporarily, and other lagging factors will be found in the economic and institutional environment. In the transition period, market imperfections arise from a slow development of financial markets, business and marketing services, infrastructure, as well as from an inadequate legal order. The task of specific measures is to make the structural adjustment easier and faster, thereby creating an upward shift of line BB in Figure 8-1.

In line with the comparative nature of this study, no detailed recommendations can be made with respect to appropriate SMI promotion policies for individual countries. However, specific areas are identified in which government assistance may be warranted, and some crucial elements concerning the design of supportive measures are outlined tentatively.

Financial assistance: From the discussion in Chapter 6, it follows that the objective of providing financial assistance to SMIs is to put into gear a process of mutual approach during which transaction costs of lending are reduced. Experience and improved screening procedures of financial institutions as well as better documentation and familiarity with lending procedures of SMI borrowers will both contribute to this goal. Financial liberalization alone is unlikely to bring about such a development in the short and medium run for two reasons. First, interest rates would initially have to rise to very high levels to make lending to SMIs profitable. At such high interest rates, demand for loans would be very low and default risks eventually higher than at lower rates [10]. In order to achieve the long-term gains of increased SMI lending, financial institutions would have to charge interest rates that do not fully reflect administrative costs and default risks, and be prepared to incur initial losses in lending to SMIs. Uncertain gains in the future and a short-term horizon on the side of banks make this option rather unlikely. Secondly, there would be the tendency for individual banks not to incur the initial costs involved in improving the capabilities of SMI borrowers to deal with financial institutions in the expectation that other such institutions would make such an investment (isolation paradox). For these two reasons, financial assistance seems to be justified.

It is nevertheless difficult to decide how financial assistance should be designed. One option consists of interest rate subsidies supplemented by an optional credit insurance scheme. Interest rate subsidies differ from concessional lending because financial institutions retain their flexibility to charge cost covering

interest rates to individual SMI borrowers. This subsidy could take the form of a preferential refinancing
facility for SMI credits with the size of the subsidy
such that lending costs are reduced to a point equal to
low-risk SMI borrowers. The subsidy also could decrease
with plant size. Optional credit insurance combines the
advantages of lower transaction costs and improved
access of collateral deficient borrowers to formal
credit. Simultaneously, an optional scheme provides an
incentive for financial institutions to develop screening procedures that would reduce the need for risk
insurance.

While such a combination of interest rate subsidies
and insurance schemes would be flexible enough to
provide potential access to institutional finance for a
wide range of SMI borrowers, it may be argued that
these incentives are not sufficient to overcome the
initial reluctance of financial institutions to provide
SMI financing. If such institutional rigidities exist
in individual countries, mandatory lending to SMIs - as
applied in Malaysia - could be considered. However, the
relative success of such regulations in the case of
Malaysia seems to be related to the high level of
financial development already achieved in that country.
In countries with less-developed financial institutions
and markets, technical assistance programs appear to be
preferable as they directly address the reasons for the
reluctance of financial institutions. Technical assistance should be provided to both sides of the market,
i.e. staff training and the development of appropriate
procedures for financial institutions, and assistance
in formulating feasibility studies and loan applications for SMIs. How effective such programs can be was
shown above with reference to SEDP in Indonesia and
MASICAP in the Philippines. Analyses of these programs
suggest, however, that more funds would have to be
allocated to them in order to assist a significant
number of SMIs.

Another element of financial assistance to SMIs
should be improvements in the legal system. In many
countries it is extremely difficult to take legal
action against delinquent borrowers. Improvements in
this area would not only reduce the risk for lenders
but would also deter some high-risk borrowers. Similarly, a proper documentation of land titles could improve
the collateral position of many small entrepreneurs.

Business services: It has been argued above that a
plant size bias in economic policies tends to impede
expansion of the supply of private business services.
However, when the plant size bias is reduced, additional supply is unlikely to be created in the short run.
Government action is required, first, to meet the imme-
diate demand of SMIs for such services and, secondly,
to facilitate the establishment of business services on

a private basis. As a first step, advisory services as
well as assistance in product development and design,
quality control and related fields may be offered by
public agencies charging relatively moderate fees. Some
degree of subsidization may be warranted initially
because of the positive externalities created by extension services. As a second step, fees may be raised to
commercial levels for second-time customers. Thus,
negative repercussions on the development of private
supply can be greatly reduced. As a third step, public
service centers may be confined to problem identification and referral to specialized private consultants.
It should be considered whether service centers can be
established as departments of semipublic industrial
associations; such agencies may have a comparative
advantage in providing specialized information.

A similar line of reasoning applies to the development of marketing services. Despite potential demand,
lack of such services may preclude the participation of
many SMIs in interregional and international trade.
Possible government actions in this field are manifold
and range from facilitating subcontracting to the promotion of trading firms. The latter may be especially
successful in export marketing of SMI products. Trading
firms can become suppliers of working capital and raw
materials, and can provide advice in technical fields
as well as in product development and design. On
account of the externalities thus created, some initial
subsidization may be justified in order to promote
closer ties between SMIs and trading houses. As a further element of a marketing assistance package, SMIs
should be given due consideration in government procurement.

Infrastructure: Nontraditional SMIs in particular
are highly dependent on a reliable external supply of
public utilities and on other infrastructural facilities. When the growth potential of SMIs is increased
by a reduction of the plant size bias in macroeconomic
policies, more and better infrastructural facilities
are required to mobilize this potential and eventually
improve the regional dispersion of industrial activities. An economical way of providing such facilities
may be industrial estates or flatted factory buildings
close to residential areas [11]. Besides the realiza-
tion of economies of scale in providing infrastructural
facilities, there are further advantages of grouping
many SMIs together locationally. The provision of
buildings on a rental basis will ease financial problems and lower overhead costs for individual SMIs, and
marketing and other types of technical assistance can
be provided more easily and at lower cost. A cross-
fertilization of ideas may be facilitated among SMI
entrepreneurs in industrial estates and the establishment of industrial associations is encouraged, which

could better articulate SMI demands in political processes. Demand for factory space or sites in industrial
estates, which has been sluggish in the past, can be
expected to expand once a favorable economic environment for SMI development is created.

NOTES

1. This point is also stressed by Marsden (1981, p.
14).
2. Most of the literature on SMIs in developing
countries argues along these lines. A fairly represen-
tative sample would include Staley, Morse (1965); World
Bank (1978a); Sharma (1979); Bolnick (1982).
3. Subcontracting, for example, is encouraged in
the Philippines, to date, however, with somewhat dis-
couraging results.
4. See e.g. Anderson (1982, pp. 32 ff.).
5. See MASICAP (1979).
6. See Bauer (1981, pp. 185 ff.). This view also
follows from Hayek (1979, Vol. 3, Ch. 15).
7. See e.g. Krueger (1978).
8. See Cortes, Ishaq (1981, p. 8).
9. In the same instance, some traditional establishments and inefficient SMIs may, however, be eliminated.
10. This possibility arises since projects, which
are potentially viable even at high interest rates,
tend to be risky projects. See Anderson (1982).
11. Such flatted factory buildings have been con-
structed in Singapore. Closeness to residential areas
is important, because many workers in SMIs are women,
requiring flexibility in work organization and easy
commuting.

9
Summary of Main Findings

The development of small- and medium-scale industries is generally believed to be a substantial contribution in developing countries to employment creation
and generation of income, particularly for low-income
population groups. The purpose of this study was to
evaluate the actual and potential importance of SMIs in
employment, income and output growth in ASEAN countries, the majority of which face difficulties in providing adequate employment for their rapidly increasing
labor forces. Differences in the actual performances of
SMIs among countries were traced to differences of
relative economic efficiency and to the respective
economic environments in which SMIs operate, including
the macroeconomic framework created by the respective
development strategy pursued by individual countries as
well as specific SMI promotion policies applied in
these countries.

The evidence available for the 1970s shows substantial differences in employment and value added shares
among ASEAN countries as well as between ASEAN
countries and industrialized countries in which SMIs
continue to play an important role in manufacturing
production. Cottage and household industries (defined
as establishments with one to nine persons engaged) are
extremely important in terms of their employment shares
in Indonesia and also in the Philippines, but much less
so in Malaysia and Singapore. In Malaysia, the share of
CIs in employment, value added, and value of production
is even smaller than in Japan, but still larger than in
the United States. The respective shares of small-scale
industries defined as establishments with 10-49 persons
engaged in employment (with the exception of Indonesia)
and value added are far smaller in the ASEAN countries
than in Japan. This is especially pronounced for the
Philippines, where the share of SIs in value added is
even less than in the United States. This is not the
case, however, for medium-scale industries (defined as
establishments with 50-99 persons engaged), and the
Philippines can be regarded as an example for a highly

dualistic manufacturing sector with a large number of labor-intensive CIs on one side, and a large number of large-scale establishments on the other. Quite differently, SIs and MIs are well represented in the Malaysian manufacturing sector. Because of its many labor-intensive LIs, Singapore takes an intermediate position, while in Indonesia the share of LIs in employment is relatively low, but the share in value added relatively high. These differences in the importance of the SMI sector among ASEAN countries reflect not only the different levels of economic development, but also the competition between small-scale and large-scale enterprises in their specific economic environments.

The competitiveness of SMIs is influenced by the efficiency of resource use in their operations. An assessment of economic efficiency of manufacturing establishments in Malaysia, the Philippines, and Singapore shows that in all countries, SMIs prove to be economically more efficient than larger establishments in approximately half of the 24 industrial subsectors included in the analysis. Within the SMI sector, however, there are substantial differences among countries with respect to the relative efficiency of SIs and MIs. SIs are efficient only in a very small number of industrial subsectors in Malaysia and the Philippines while in the Singaporean economy there are no pronounced differences between SIs and MIs with respect to economic efficiency. Furthermore, in Singapore, SIs and MIs tend to be efficient users of resources in industries in which only MIs and LIs respectively are economically efficient in the other two countries.

The latter observation and the productivity differentials between SMIs in developed and developing countries suggest that SMIs can significantly contribute to industrial growth and employment creation only if they succeed in upgrading their technology and in adjusting their product mix continuously. Traditional SMIs using simple technologies and producing simple consumer goods for low-income consumers gradually have to give way to modern SMIs that are suppliers of industrial intermediates and viable exporters of manufactured goods. Whether structural adjustment within the SMI sector is enhanced or impeded depends on incentives or disincentives to SMI development provided by the applied industrialization strategies.

The assessment of economic efficiency provides only a static view since the analysis is based on prevailing prices. These prices are influenced by the trade, investment and credit policies applied in individual countries and by sector-specific policies such as SMI promotion schemes. An evaluation of these policies leads to several general conclusions. First, the structure of effective protection (EPR) in ASEAN countries (except Singapore) seems to have benefitted LIs more than SMIs; LIs are concentrated in industries with relatively high EPRs, while SMIs and CIs are concentrated in industries with relatively low or negative EPRs. Second, selective measures tend to aggravate the policy-induced discrimination of SMIs via-a-vis LIs within individual industries. Such measures comprise foreign exchange and import controls, selective tariff protection on a case-by-case basis, exemptions from import duties, tax incentives, and subsidized export credit. Third, the protective system as well as additional selective measures have had negative effects on the growth potential of SMIs by impeding improvements in product quality and output mix as well as by reducing domestic final and intermediate demand for SMI products.

This policy bias against SMIs was aggravated when financial institutions preferred lending to well-established large-scale establishments as a result of interventionistic credit policies. Reduced access of SMIs to formal credit was largely the consequence of regulated interest rate spreads too narrow to cover the transaction costs associated with SMI lending. High transaction costs for SMI lending reflect a lack of mutual familiarity between financial institutions and SMIs. SMI promotion policies have by and large not been able to offset the policy-induced biases in favor of large establishments for several reasons.

In Indonesia, the Philippines, and especially in Thailand, financial assistance to SMIs has remained too small in quantitative terms to offset the lack of access to formal credit, which is at least partly a consequence of monetary and credit policies pursued in these countries. In the comparatively liberal financial environment prevailing in Malaysia and in Singapore, access to formal credit is much less of a problem for SMIs than in the other ASEAN countries, despite the small scale of financial assistance granted to SMIs in these two countries. This comparison shows that access to formal credit does not necessarily depend on financial assistance programs and that concessional interest rates are not an indispensible element of SMI promotion policies. Low interest ceilings and fixed interest rate spreads tend to benefit larger borrowers with sufficient collateral at the expense of economically profitable projects where little collateral can be offered. Credit insurance schemes applied in several countries have done little to prevent this bias.

The financing programs have undeniably improved the climate for SMI lending by supporting the accumulation of information and experience with respect to this kind of lending activities by both banks and SMI customers. The accumulation of experience was enhanced, however, more by technical assistance programs than through concessional financing schemes as such. The potential created by improved knowledge and information was exploited only when banks were given freedom to adjust lending terms to their perception of the risks involved.

The review of SMI promotion policies suggests that both financial and nonfinancial assistance to SMIs was neither sufficient in quantitative terms nor appropriate in design to compensate for the discrimination inherent in macroeconomic policies. The impediments to SMI development are reflected in establishment characteristics analyzed at the micro level. The evidence shows clearly that the viability of the SMI sector depends on changes in restrictive macroeconomic policies. However, such policy changes would have to be supplemented by appropriately designed SMI support schemes if the economic environment of SMIs is to be improved significantly. Such specific SMI policies can be justified economically since they help to overcome market imperfections and to facilitate economic adjustment to changing macroeconomic parameters. Although detailed recommendations for SMI promotion policies warrant further country analysis, a number of general suggestions can be derived from the experience of ASEAN countries.

The objective of financial assistance to SMIs should be to trigger a mechanism that will improve access of SMIs to formal credit beyond financial assistance schemes. This objective can be achieved by providing interest rate spreads that make SMI lending more attractive to commercial and state banks. When SMI lending is not yet established, transaction costs are high and competition among commercial banks is weak as banks cannot be expected to cross-subsidize SMI lending from their own initiative. They will require at least initial encouragement to increase their familiarity with SMI borrowers and to develop lending procedures. This encouragement could be provided through preferential refinancing facilities combined with optional credit risk insurance and interest rates for SMI loans allowed to adjust to the perceived credit risks. Such a combination of measures would facilitate access of new or high-risk SMI borrowers to formal credit and would also include an interest rate subsidy for SMIs compared to market rates.

The process of familiarizing financial institutions and SMI customers would be greatly helped by technical assistance programs supporting both SMIs and commercial banks in project selection and appraisal. The merits of such programs are evident from experiences in Indonesia and the Philippines. Other nonfinancial assistance measures suited to promote SMI development concern the supply of business services such as technological, managerial and marketing assistance, telecommunications, infrastructure and public utilities, and an adequate supply of sites for factories. Some of these services may be offered by private suppliers or trading companies, but SMIs are not likely to be reached by these services for various reasons. Therefore, in the initial phase, nonfinancial assistance should be provided at subsidized rates by government agencies. However, such measures should not simply substitute private services, but should bridge the gap between SMIs and private suppliers of services.

There are two major lessons in this study to be learned by policy makers in developing countries. First, it shows the manifold interdependencies between general development strategies and the viability of the SMI sectors. These links between micro and macro levels are inescapable, and no government budget would be large enough to compensate SMIs fully for disincentives inherent in misguided trade, industrialization or monetary policies. Second, in a conducive environment SMIs can contribute significantly to economic development not only by offering additional employment and income particularly to less privileged parts of the workforce, but perhaps even more importantly, by acting as links in the chain of intra-industrial linkages which are preconditions for establishing an internationally competitive manufacturing industry.

References

Akrasanee, Narongchai (1977), Industrial Development in Thailand. Report prepared for the World Bank. Thammasat University, Bangkok, September, mimeo.

Akrasanee, Narongchai (1978), Trade Strategy for Employment Growth in Thailand. Council for Asian Manpower Studies, Discussion Papers, 78-16, Quezon City, August.

Anderson, Dennis (1982), Small Industry in Developing Countries: Some Issues. World Bank, Staff Working Papers, 518, Washington, D.C.

Anderson, Dennis, Farida Khambata, (1981), Small Enterprises and Development Policy in the Philippines: A Case Study. World Bank, Staff Working Papers, 468, Washington, D.C.

Anderson-Saito, Katrine, Delano P. Villanueva (1981), "Transaction Costs of Credit to the Small-Scale Sector in the Philippines". Economic Development and Cultural Change, Vol. 29, pp. 631-640.

Arief, K. (1981), Small Scale Enterprise and Small Enterprise Credit Programs in Indonesia: Background and Experience. Paper prepared for "Asian Regional Meeting of Donor Agencies on Small Scale Enterprise Development, Colombo, December 8-11, 1981". World Bank, Industrial Development and Finance Department, Washington, D.C., mimeo.

Arndt, Heinz W. (1979), "Monetary Policy Instruments in Indonesia". Bulletin of Indonesian Economic Studies, Vol. 15, 3, pp. 107-122.

Asian Development Bank by Economic Office Staff under the direction of Seiji Naya (1982), Developing Asia: The Importance of Domestic Policies. Manila, 9.

Baldwin, Robert E. (1975), Foreign Trade Regimes and Economic Development. National Bureau of Economic Research, New York.

Bank Negara Malaysia, Annual Report and Statement of Accounts. Kuala Lumpur, various issues.

Bank Negara Malaysia (1979), Money and Banking in Malaysia. Kuala Lumpur.

Bauer, Peter Tamas (1981), Equality, the Third World and Economic Delusion. London.

Bautista, Romeo, John H. Power and Associates (1979), Industrial Promotion Policies in the Philippines. Philippine Institute for Development Studies, Manila.

Board of Investment (Thailand) (1979), List of Activities Eligible for Promotion (Compiled as of December 31, 1979). Bangkok.

Bolnick, Bruce (1982), "Concessional Credit for Small Scale Enterprise". Bulletin of Indonesian Economic Studies, Vol. 18, 2, pp. 65-85.

Bruch, Mathias (1980), "Small Enterprises as Exporters of Manufactures: Tentative Evidence from Malaysia". World Development, Oxford, Vol. 8, pp. 429-442.

Bruch, Mathias (1982a), Lohnsatzdifferenzen zwischen großen und kleinen Industriebetrieben: Eine Untersuchung für die ASEAN-Länder (Wage Rate Differentials between Large and Small Industrial Establishments: An Analysis for ASEAN Countries). Kiel Institute of World Economics, Kiel Working Papers, 137.

Bruch, Mathias (1982b), Zur Finanzierung kleiner Industriebetriebe in den ASEAN-Ländern (Financing Small Industrial Establishments in ASEAN Countries). Kiel Institute of World Economics, Kiel Working Papers, 138.

Bruch, Mathias (1982c), Kleinbetriebe und Industrialisierungspolitik in Entwicklungsländern - Eine vergleichende Analyse der ASEAN-Länder (Small-Scale Establishments and Industrialization Policies in Developing Countries - A Comparative Analysis for ASEAN Countries). Kieler Studien, 182, Tübingen 1983.

Chee Peng Lim (1975), The Role of Small Industry in the Malaysian Economy. Diss., University of Malaya, Kuala Lumpur.

Chee Peng Lim, Foong Wai Fong (1979), An Analysis of Small Industry in Malaysia. ARTEP's Project on ASEAN Comparative Study of Labour-Intensive Industries in Malaysia. University of Malaya, Kuala Lumpur, September, mimeo.

Chee Peng Lim, Mavis C. Puthucheary, Donald Lee (1979), A Study of Small Entrepreneurs and Entrepreneurial Development Programmes in Malaysia. University of Malaya, Kuala Lumpur.

Cortes, M., A. Ishaq (1981), Determinants of Economic Performance and Technical Efficiency in Colombian Small and Medium Enterprises. World Bank, Washington, D.C., January, mimeo.

Donges, Juergen B., Bernd Stecher, Frank Wolter (1974), Industrial Development Policies for Indonesia. Kieler Studien, 126, Tübingen.

Economic Development Board (EDB) (1961-1979/80), Annual Report. Singapore.

Gregorio, Rosario G. (1979), "An Economic Analysis of the Effects of Philippine Fiscal Incentives for Industrial Promotion". In: Romeo M. Bautista, John H. Power and Associates, Industrial Promotion Policies in the Philippines. Philippine Institute for Development Studies, Manila, pp. 173-240.

Griliches, Zvi (1967), "Production Functions in Manufacturing: Some Preliminary Results". In: Murray Brown (Ed.), The Theory and Empirical Analysis of Production. National Bureau of Economic Research. New York, London, pp. 275-322.

Hayek, Friedrich August von (1979), Law, Legislation, and Liberty, Vol. 3 (The Political Order of a Free People), Chicago.

Hiemenz, Ulrich (1982), Industrial Growth and Employment in Developing Asian Countries: Issues and Perspectives for the Coming Decade. Asian Development Bank Economics Staff Paper, 7, Manila, March.

Hill, Hal C. (1979), Choice of Technique in the Indonesian Weaving Industry. Diss., Australian National University, Canberra, December.

Hill, Hal C. (1981), Subcontracting and Technological Diffusion in Philippine Manufacturing. University of the Philippines, Discussion Papers, 8112, Manila.

Ho, Sam P.S. (1980), Small-Scale Enterprises in Korea and Taiwan. World Bank, Staff Working Papers, 384, Washington, D.C.

Hoffmann, Lutz, Tan Siew Ee (1980), Industrial Growth, Employment and Foreign Investment in Peninsular Malaysia. Oxford.

International Development Center of Japan (1977/78), Industrial Development in Southeast Asian Countries: Small- and Medium-Scale Industries - Republic of Indonesia, Phase I. Tokyo.

International Monetary Fund (IMF) (1980), International Financial Statistics Yearbook, Washington, D.C.

International Monetary Fund (IMF), International Financial Statistics, June 1983.

Itao, A. F. (1980), "A Study of Mortality Rates and Causes of Failure of Small-Scale Industries in the Philippines". University of the Philippines Institute for Small-Scale Industries (UPISSI), Manila.

Krueger, Anne O. (1978), "Foreign Trade Regimes and Economic Development: Liveralization Attempts and Consequences". New York, Cambridge/Mass.

128

Leibenstein, Harvey (1968), "Entrepreneurship and Development". The American Economic Review, Vol. 58, pp. 72-83.

Lim, Linda, Pang Eng Fong (1981), Vertical Linkages and Multinational Enterprises in Developing Countries. National University of Singapore, mimeo.

Marsden, K., (1981), "Creating the Right Environment for Small Firms", Finance and Development, Vol. 18, 4, pp. 33-36.

McCawley, Peter (1979), Industrialization in Indonesia: Developments and Prospects. Australian National University, Occasional Papers, 13, Canberra.

McCawley, Peter, Maree Tait (1979), "New Data on Employment in Manufacturing 1970-76." Bulletin of Indonesian Economic Studies, Vol. 15, 1, pp. 125-136.

Medium- and Small-Scale Industries Coordinated Action Program (MASICAP) (1979), Report of the Monitoring of MASICAP-Assisted Projects. Information Analysis Unit, Bureau of Small and Medium Industries (BSMI), Manila, mimeo.

Minami, Ryoshin (1976), "The Introduction of Electrical Power and Its Impact on the Manufacturing Industries: With Special Reference to Smaller Scale Plants". In: Hugh Patrick (Ed.), Japanese Industrialization and Its Social Consequences. Berkeley, pp. 299-326.

Morawetz, David (1974), "Employment Implications of Industrialization in Developing Countries: A Survey". The Economic Journal, Vol. 84, pp. 491-542.

National Cottage Industries Development Agency (NACIDA), NACIDA-Primer. Manila, undated, mimeo.

Nelson, Richard, T. Paul Schultz, Robert L. Slighton (1971), Structural Change in a Developing Economy: Columbia's Problems and Prospects. Princeton/N.J.

Page, John M. Jr. (1980), "Technical Efficiency and Economic Performance: Some Evidence from Ghana", Oxford Economic Papers,Vol. 23, 2, pp. 319-339.

Pitt, Mark M. (1981), "Alternative Trade Strategies and Employment in Indonesia". In: Anne O. Krueger, Hal B. Lary, Terry Monson, Narongchai Akrasanee (Eds.), Trade and Employment in Developing Countries. Chicago, pp. 181-238.

Power, John H., Gerardo P. Sicat (1971), Industry and Trade in Some Developing Countries: The Philippines, Industrialization and Trade Policies. Organisation for Economic Co-operation and Development, Development Centre, London.

Rabenau, Kurt von (1976), "Trade Policies and Industrialization in a Developing Country: The Case of West Malaysia". The Malayan Economic Review, Vol. 21, pp. 23-46.

Rhee, Yung (1980), Incentive Systems and Policies for the Manufacturing Industries in Malaysia. World Bank, Washington, D.C., mimeo.

Roepke, Jochen (1979), "Entrepreneurship and Economic Development in Indonesia". Prisma, Jakarta, 13, pp. 51-66.

Sanguanruang, Saeng, Nisa Xuto, Preeyanuch Saengpassorn, Chucheep Piputsitee (1978), Development of Small and Medium Manufacturing Enterpises in Thailand. Association of Development Research and Training Institutes of Asia and the Pacific. ADIPA Research Project, Vol. 1, Main Report, Bangkok.

Shalit, Sol. S, U. Sankar (1977), "The Measurement of Firm Size". The Review of Economics and Statistics, Vol. 59, pp. 290-298.

Sharma, S.V.S. (1979), Small Entrepreneurial Development in Some Asian Countries. New Delhi.

Shaw, Edward S. (1973), Financial Deepening in Economic Development. Economic Development Series, New York.

Singapore International Chamber of Commerce (1979), Investor's Guide, Singapore, August.

Sit, V.F.S., S.L. Wong, T.S. Kiang (1979), "Small-Scale Industry in a Laissez-Faire Economy: A Hong Kong Case Study". Centre of Asian Studies, Unversity of Hong Kong.

Spinanger, Dean (1980), Regional Industrialization Policies in a Small Developing Country. A Case Study of West Malaysia. Kiel Institute of World Economics. Kiel.

Staley, Eugene (1958), Small Industry Development. Stanford Research Institute, Research Programme on Small Industry Development, Miscellaneous Paper, 1, Menlo Park, Calif.

Staley, Eugene, Richard Morse (1965), Modern Small Industry of Developing Countries. New York.

Tambunlertchai, Somsak, Chesada Loohawenchit (1980), Labour-Intensive and Small-Scale Manufacturing Industries in Thailand. Paper presented at the Seminar on ASEAN Comparative Study of the Development of Labour-Intensive Industry, ILO-ARTEP (International Labour Organization - Asian Regional Team for Employment Promotion), Bangkok, October.

Tan, Norma A. (1979), "The Structure of Protection and Resource Flows in the Philippines". In: Romeo M. Bautista, John H. Power and Associates, Industrial Promotion Policies and the Philippines. Philippine Institute for Development Studies,Manila, pp. 127-172.

Tan Siew Ee (1979), Labour Market Developments of Peninsular Malaysia: Problems and Perspectives. Diss., University of Regensburg.

DiTullio, Kathleen A. (1974), "Small Enterprises in Manufacturing: The Emerging Issues". In: Organisation for Economic Co-operation and Development (OECD), Development Centre, Transfer of Technology for Small Industries. Paris, pp. 78-100.

United Nations (UN) (1979), The 1973 World Programme of Industrial Statistics, Summary of Data from Selected Countries. New York.

University of the Philippines Institute for Small-Scale Industries (UPISSI) (1979), Entrepreneurship and Small Enterprises Development: The Philippine Experience. Quezon City.

van der Veen, J.H. (1977), Promoting Small-Scale Industries: The Role of the Asian Development Bank. Asian Development Bank, Economic Office, Occasional Paper, 9, Manila, June.

Visanuvimol, Vilai (1980), Export Incentives and the Development of Manufactured Exports in Thailand: A Quantitative Study. Thammasat University, Bangkok, June.

Warr, Peter George (1981), Sub-optimal Saving and the Shadow Price of Labor. Australian National University, Canberra, August, mimeo.

Watanabe, Susumu (1979), Technical Co-Operation between Large and Small Firms in the Filipino Automobile Industry. International Labour Organisation, World Employment Programme, Working Paper WEP 2-22/WP 47, Geneva.

World Bank (1978a), Employment and Development of Small Enterprises. Sector Policy Paper, Washington, D.C.

World Bank (1978b), World Development Report 1978. Washington, D.C.

World Bank (1980), The Philippines, Aspects of the Financial Sector. A Joint World Bank/IMF Study, Washington, D.C.

Yin, Koh F., David H. Clark (1976), "Labor Absorption and Economic Growth in Singapore". The Philippine Economic Journal, Vol. 15, 1 and 2, pp. 314-342.